WHAT YOU NEED TO KNOW ABOUT SPIRITUAL WARFARE

12 LESSONS THAT CAN CHANGE YOUR LIFE

MAX ANDERS

AUTHOR OF *30 DAYS TO UNDERSTANDING THE BIBLE*

3/2013

THOMAS NELSON
Since 1798

NASHVILLE   DALLAS   MEXICO CITY   RIO DE JANEIRO

© 1997 by Max Anders

Published in Nashville, Tennessee, by Thomas Nelson, Inc.

Library of Congress Cataloging-in-Publication Data

Anders, Max E., 1947–

    What You Need to Know About Spiritual Warfare/Max Anders.

    Includes bibliographical references.

    ISBN 978-1-4185-4854-4

    1. Spiritual warfare.   I. Title.   II. Series.

BV4501.2.A456 1997

235′.4—dc20

97–12964

CIP

Printed in the United States of America

11 12 13 14 15 QG 05 04 03 02 01

CONTENTS

INTRODUCTION TO THE
WHAT YOU NEED TO KNOW SERIES

You hold in your hands a tool with enormous potential—the ability to help ground you, and a whole new generation of other Christians, in the basics of the Christian faith.

I believe the times call for just this tool. We face a serious crisis in the church today . . . namely, a generation of Christians who know the truth but who do not live it. An even greater challenge is coming straight at us, however: a coming generation of Christians who may not even know the truth!

Many Christian leaders agree that today's evangelical church urgently needs a tool flexible enough to be used by a wide variety of churches to ground current and future generations of Christians in the basics of Scripture and historic Christianity.

This guide, and the whole series from which it comes—the *What You Need to Know* series—can be used by individuals or groups for just that reason.
Here are five other reasons why we believe you will enjoy using this guide:

1. It is easy to read.

You don't want to wade through complicated technical jargon to try to stumble on the important truths you are looking for. This series puts biblical truth right out in the open. It is written in a warm and friendly style, with even a smattering of humor here and there. See if you don't think it is different from anything you have ever read before.

2. It is easy to teach.

You don't have time to spend ten hours preparing for Sunday school, small group, or discipleship lessons. On the other hand, you don't want watered-down material that insults your group's intellect. There is real meat in these pages, but it is presented in a way that is easy to teach. It follows a question-and-answer format that can be used to cover the material, along with discussion questions at the end of each chapter that make it easy to get group interaction going.

3. It is thoroughly biblical.

You believe the Bible, and don't want to use anything that isn't thoroughly biblical. This series has been written and reviewed by a team of well-educated, personally committed Christians who have a high view of Scripture, and great care has been taken to reflect what the Bible teaches. If the Bible is unambiguous on a subject, such as the resurrection of Christ, then that subject is presented unambiguously.

4. It respectfully presents differing evangelical positions.

You don't want anyone forcing conclusions on you that you don't agree with. There are many subjects in the Bible on which there is more than one responsible position. When that is the case, this series presents those positions with respect, accuracy, and fairness. In fact, to make sure, a team of evaluators from various evangelical perspectives has reviewed each of the volumes in this series.

5. It lets you follow up with your own convictions and distinctives on a given issue.

You may have convictions on an issue that you want to communicate to the people to whom you are ministering. These books give you that flexibility. After presenting the various responsible positions that may be held on a given subject, you will then find it easy to identify and expand upon your view, or the view of your church.

We send this study guide to you with the prayer that God may use it to help strengthen His church for her work in these days.

HOW TO TEACH THIS BOOK

The books in this series are written so that they can be used as a thirteen-week curriculum, ideal for Sunday school classes or other small group meetings. You will notice that there are only twelve chapters—to allow for a session when you may want to do something else. Every quarter seems to call for at least one different type of session, because of holidays, summer vacation, or other special events. If you use all twelve chapters, and still have a session left in the quarter, have a fellowship meeting with refreshments, and use the time to get to know others better. Or use the session to invite newcomers in hopes they will continue with the course.

All ten books in the series together form a "Basic Knowledge Curriculum" for Christians. Certainly, Christians would eventually want to know more than is in these books, but they should not know less. Therefore, the series is excellent for seekers, for new Christians, and for Christians who may not have a solid foundation of biblical education. It is also a good series for those whose biblical education has been spotty.

Of course, the books can also be used in small groups and discipleship groups. If you are studying the book by yourself, you can simply read the chapters and go through the material at the end. If you are using the books to teach others, you might find the following guidelines helpful:

Teaching Outline

1. Begin the session with prayer.

2. Consider having a quiz at the beginning of each meeting over the self-test from the chapter to be studied for that day. The quiz can be optional, or the group may want everyone to commit to it, depending on the setting in which the material is taught. In a small discipleship group or one-on-one, it might be required. In a larger Sunday school class, it might need to be optional.

3. At the beginning of the session, summarize the material. You may want to have class members be prepared to summarize the material. You might want to bring in information that was not covered in the book. There might be some in the class who have not read the material, and this will help catch them up with those who did. Even for those who did read it, a summary will refresh their minds and get everyone into a common mind-set. It may also generate questions and discussion.

4. Discuss the material at the end of the chapters as time permits. Use whatever you think best fits the group.

5. Have a special time for questions and answers, or encourage questions during the course of discussion. If you are asked a question you can't answer (it happens to all of us), just say you don't know, but that you will find out. Then, the following week, you can open the question-and-answer time, or perhaps the discussion time, with the answer to the question from last week.

6. Close with prayer.

You may have other things you would like to incorporate, and flexibility is the key to success. These suggestions are given only to guide, not to dictate. Prayerfully choose a plan suited to your circumstances.

1

WHAT IS SPIRITUAL WARFARE?

Do you really want to see divine power at work? Then discard your human notions of power and look at the way Christ lived and died.
—**Edmund A. Steimle**

For over two hundred years, Benedict Arnold has been cussed and discussed as an unfaithful American. Why? Because during the War for Independence, he attempted to smuggle a diagram of the fort at West Point on the Hudson River to the British enemy. Succeeding generations of Americans have never forgiven him for his act of treason, and Arnold's name has entered our language as a synonym for *traitor*.

"Why would Arnold do such a thing?" countless history students have asked. "What possessed one of the finest generals in the American army to defect?" Well, let me tell you another side to the story. The recent discovery of letters between Arnold and Benjamin Franklin has shed new light on the reasoning behind his treasonous act.

The desperate American colonies had asked the French for help in their battle with the British. The French, glad to oblige, sent so many troops across the Atlantic that at one time, the French soldiers fighting outnumbered the American troops they were helping.

General Arnold became deeply suspicious of the French motives. Why would the French be so willing to spill so much of their own blood on behalf of the Americans? Was their plan perhaps to help the Americans defeat the British and then make America a French colony instead? Arnold wrote to Franklin that America was going to be a colony of either Great Britain or France. If that were the case, Arnold preferred British rule. By remaining a British colony, America would be ruled rather benevolently and the thirteen colonies might eventually be given their freedom. If they became a French colony, they would be ruled by tyrants and never given their independence. Therefore, Arnold argued, the American colonies should sue for peace with England.

Franklin, who was ambassador to France at the time, agreed with Arnold's opinions. Nevertheless, he said, "I believe, in the sovereignty of God, it will somehow work out." Franklin strongly opposed any overtures for peace with the British.

Benedict Arnold, however, was not content to entrust so much to the sovereignty of God. As far as he was concerned, the way to attain the great dream of freedom was to help the British win. Therefore, in an act of what Arnold would have described as deep patriotism, he attempted to turn the diagram of West Point over to the British. When that failed, he joined the British, not to conquer the colonies, but, as he saw it, to defeat the French and drive them off American soil.

As this story shows, warfare is not just armies on opposite sides of a line drawn in the sand having at it. Warfare is also diplomacy, espionage, negotiations, and maneuvering behind the scenes—which at times can have a greater impact on the outcome than the fighting on the battlefront. Because, after all, what's really at stake is power.

Whether they know it or not, all Christians are engaged in a titanic spiritual battle, not against the forces of any earthly nation, but against the forces of darkness. Yet this battle is largely unseen . . . an invisible war. Things go on behind the scenes that we do not naturally perceive or understand. Yet these invisible acts and forces often determine spiritual victories or defeats. We must understand spiritual warfare if we are to emerge spiritually victorious.

This war is between good and bad, between righteousness and evil, between truth and falsehood. God is the source of all good, and with Him are good angels and His people. The initiator of evil is Satan, and he is allied with demons

IN THIS CHAPTER WE LEARN THAT . . .

1. The three battlefronts in our spiritual warfare are the world, the flesh, and the devil.

2. The source of our strength in the spiritual war is God alone.

3. Our weapons of war are the pieces of spiritual armor described in Scripture.

4. Satan employs two particularly effective means of deceiving us: first, he gets us to sin; then, once we have sinned, he keeps us mired in guilt.

5. We are able to overcome by realizing that his only power over us is that of deception and fear, and by resisting him God's way.

6. The three primary perspectives on spiritual warfare are the Spiritual Resistance View, the Truth Encounter View, and the Power Encounter View.

and all those whom Satan can deceive into serving his purposes. God's purpose is to fill all of creation with His glory. So He works to advance righteousness, goodness, peace, love, and joy, and to call people to believe in Him and become citizens of heaven even while they live on earth. Satan's purpose is to spoil all of creation and to deny and oppose God's glory however he can, so Satan advances sin, evil, hatred, and despair, and seeks to prevent people from believing in God and becoming citizens of heaven. God's strategy is to enlighten and save. Satan's strategy is to deceive and destroy.

WHAT ARE THE THREE BATTLEFRONTS IN SPIRITUAL WARFARE?

The three battlefronts in our spiritual warfare are the world, the flesh, and the devil.

Spiritual warfare occurs in our everyday lives in different ways, sometimes blatantly, but often very subtly. The rest of the book explores these ways. The Bible shows that this conflict rages on three battlefronts. These fronts are the world (1 John 2:15–17), the flesh (Romans 7:14–25), and the devil (1 Peter 5:8).

The "world" does not mean the material planet. This physical world was created by God, and He pronounced it good (Genesis 1). Yes, it has been corrupted by sin, but it will be redeemed and made new (Romans 8:19–22; Revelation 21:1) and be totally good again. That is one wonderful result of the salvation God is performing today. But "world" in its negative sense is the world system of values. It is the present evil order and arrangement of things that began not with creation, but with the spoiling of God's good creation by sin (Genesis 3).

> God's purpose is to fill all of creation with His glory.

The world is the *social* battlefront, where believers battle sin and evil confronting them from "without." It is a battleground of external powers, values, influences, and temptations. In this battle, the Bible admonishes us to be in the world but not of the world and to resist the pressure of unredeemed society that would force us into its mold (Romans 12:1–2). The apostle Paul wrote of our conflict with the world in 2 Corinthians 10:4–5, where he described worldly convictions, habits, thoughts, and affections held by society, by a culture, by humanity as a whole. These are worldly because they oppose God, deny God, or attempt to exist apart from God.

Overcoming these forces in our own lives, as well as helping others to overcome them, is part of the war we wage against the fallen world in which we live. We are to disengage ourselves from the ungodly elements of the world value system, while at the same time influencing the world for the cause of Christ (Matthew 5:14–16; 28:19–20).

The "flesh" does not mean our skin, meat, and bones, nor does it refer only to sexual desire. These are part of God's good creation. Rather, "flesh" refers to an inherent bent toward sin that every human being inherits from Adam. It refers not just to actions (sex, money, and power), but also to attitudes (lust, greed, and all kinds of selfishness). The flesh is the *personal* battlefront, where believers battle sin and evil "within" themselves, a battleground of internal powers, values, influences, and temptations.

The apostle Paul wrote of the flesh in Romans 7 where he says that "I know that in me (that is, in my flesh) nothing good dwells; for to will is present with me, but how to perform what is good I do not find. For the good that I will to do, I do not do; but the evil I will not to do, that I practice. Now if I do what I will not to do, it is no longer I who do it, but sin that dwells in me" (vv. 18-20).

This passage describes a spiritual civil war raging within the heart of each Christian. Because of the new birth in Christ, the Christian wants to do the right thing, but the flesh is not redeemed and continues to pull us down until Jesus returns or we die (Romans 8:23). So we must war against this tendency, a kind of unhealthy gravity, within ourselves pulling us against the will of God. In this battle, the Bible admonishes us not to let sin rule over our physical bodies. Instead, we are to actively present ourselves to God as instruments to be used for His righteousness (Romans 6:11–14).

The "devil" is not the little man in red tights, with hoofs, horns, and a pitchfork. He is an extremely powerful fallen angel, evil to the core, and absolutely set against God. The devil refers to a *supernatural* battlefront where believers battle Satan and other evil supernatural beings, whom the Bible identifies as the source of evil. Satan and his allies use the world and the flesh to keep us from doing the will of God.

As we consider this great invisible war in which the devil and his hosts engage us, we must concentrate on two realities. First, we are to be alert to his evil intentions, to his strategy to deceive and destroy us. Second, we must recognize that it is God alone who can make us victorious in this great invisible war. His resources, His strength, His ministry to us are what allow us to keep from being destroyed in this battle. We must develop the conviction and habit of turning to Him, depending on Him, obeying Him so that He can win the battle for us.

I realize that this is strange talk in our nuts-and-bolts world of computer chips, CDs, and space shuttles. We are not used to thinking about invisible foes and celestial combat. Yet if we are not careful, we will be duped into thinking we are merely battling people and circumstances, when all the time things are being orchestrated by a mastermind behind the scenes. The evil mastermind of darkness is intelligent and powerful. He makes archvillain Darth Vader look like child's play. If we pretend he is not there, or if we try to do battle with him in our own intelligence and strength, we are doomed to failure.

WHAT IS THE SOURCE OF OUR STRENGTH?

The source of our strength in the spiritual war is God alone.

You cannot control a flood with a flamethrower.

You cannot douse a forest fire with floodlights.

You cannot stop a hurricane with bullets. *And you cannot fight supernatural battles with natural strength.* Natural power has no effect whatsoever on spiritual things.

If we could ever get that through our heads, we would change the way we do things. Instead of relying on hard work and creativity and shrewdness and politics and money, we would rely on prayer and Scripture and godliness and spiritual unity and sensitivity to the Lord.

Our power, our strength, is only that—ours. Natural. Puny against the onslaught of Satan and his demonic army.

Of course we should work hard, be creative and shrewd, and use politics and money. But we must not depend on these things. Our true strength, our real power, does not lie within ourselves. It is in the Lord.

This is extremely difficult for us to accept at first. We may be very strong physically, accustomed to relying on our physical strength to achieve our goals. Or we may be highly skilled business executives, very talented artists, or shrewd negotiators, and we may depend on these talents to make our way through the world. So it is hard for us to lay those abilities at the foot of the cross, admit that in spiritual warfare they are useless and we are powerless, and say, "Lord Jesus, help me." But until we come to that point, we are thoroughly duped—and we will remain thoroughly defeated.

In spiritual warfare . . .

God does the work of God,

Man does the work of man.

Man cannot do the work of God,

And God will not do the work of man.

God's work—spiritual warfare—has to be done God's way. The work of humans is to learn and employ God's tactics and rely on God—and God alone—in the spiritual war.

For the life of us, however, we cannot get this straight. We insist on trying to do the work of God while neglecting the work of man. Then we wonder why things aren't going so well.

WHAT ARE THE WEAPONS OF WAR?

Our weapons of war are the pieces of spiritual armor described in Scripture.

Since we are in a spiritual battle against an invisible but very real foe, our weapons of war cannot be lead and steel. Rather, they must be spiritual weapons. And Ephesians 6 describes one of those weapons: the armor of God.

Of course, *armor* is a figure of speech, a metaphor for the spiritual resources He provides for our protection, power, and effectiveness in the spiritual warfare against the forces of darkness. These resources are truth, righteousness, the gospel of peace, faith, salvation, and the Word of God. These are the spiritual weapons for the good guys.

But this passage also tells us about the weapons of the bad guys, that is, "the schemes of the devil."

The word *schemes* in the Greek is *methodeia*, from which we derive the English word *method*. This implies craftiness, cunning, and deception—all of which describe Satan's schemes.

Both Satan's Hebrew name, *Abaddon*, and his Greek name, *Apollyon*, mean "destroyer" (Revelation 9:11). He is also called the "serpent of old, called the Devil and Satan, who deceives the whole world" (Revelation 12:9). Satan is a deceiver and a destroyer; *he deceives in order to destroy.*

In the very beginning, in the Garden of Eden, Satan deceived Adam and Eve into rebelling against God. His purpose? To destroy them. Thousands of years later, Satan attempted to deceive Jesus into departing from the will of God (Matthew 4). His goal? To destroy Him and nullify God's plan of redemption. He appears as "an angel of light" to deceive us in order to destroy us (2 Corinthians 11:14).

How does Satan deceive us? By appealing to "the lust of the flesh, the lust of the eyes, and the pride of life" (1 John 2:16), he makes

bad look good,
false appear true,
wrong look right,
ugly seem beautiful,
hurtful feel helpful,
painful look pleasant.

In every confusing, conniving, deceptive way possible, Satan attempts to mislead us with his schemes. In Matthew 24:24 we read that "false christs and false prophets will rise and show great signs and wonders to deceive, if possible, even the elect." That is how great his powers of deception and destruction are.

So you can see that by ourselves, we are no match for Satan's spiritual weapons. We need the armor of God.

The powers of darkness encompass a hierarchy of evil spiritual beings who do the bidding of their master, Satan. Difficult though it is for us to think in these terms, we must become aware of the invisible spirit world that surrounds us: forces of darkness locked in mortal combat with the forces of light. Spiritual warfare is a reality!

> **Satan deceives by arousing desires that cloud the truth and erode our loyalty to it.**

If we do not prepare for this spiritual battle, we may be the next casualty. "Be sober, be vigilant," Peter wrote, "because your adversary the devil walks about like a roaring lion, seeking whom he may devour" (1 Peter 5:8). And Paul warned that Satan transforms himself into an angel of light (2 Corinthians 11:14). Jesus asserted that Satan is "the father of lies" (John 8:44 NASB). He can make poison taste like candy. He is the master illusionist.

We engage in spiritual warfare every day, and we cannot succeed in our own strength. As soldiers of the cross we need the strength, the power—and the armor—of the Lord.

WHAT ARE SATAN'S METHODS OF DECEPTION?

Satan employs two particularly effective means of deceiving us: first, he gets us to sin; then, once we have sinned, he keeps us mired in guilt.

To get us to sin, the master of deception

convinces us that "it isn't so bad. It won't hurt,"

assures us that no one will find out, and that God will forgive us anyway,

persuades us that what he is tempting us to do will actually satisfy us,

> **Flee temptation, but fight spiritual opposition.**

saps our spiritual convictions so that we don't care,

exhausts and frazzles us so that we just want immediate relief and are willing to do whatever will give us that relief, and

twists our thinking so that we can't discern wrong from right anymore.

Spiritual conflict takes two forms: temptation and spiritual opposition. When we are tempted to sin, we are to flee (2 Timothy 2:22). When we are confronted with spiritual opposition, we are to fight (James 4:7).

Most of us, however, have a genius for reversing the two. When we sense spiritual opposition in our life and ministry, we want to flee. And when presented with temptation to sin, we want to stand and fight. That is contrary to the Word, and we will have little success until we get it straight.

Do you want to run away from your financial obligations?
    Stand and fight.
Is it too hard to improve family relationships?
    Stand and fight.
Are you tired of trying to grow spiritually?
    Stand and fight.
Is it tough being moral, ethical, and honest in the workplace?
    Stand and fight.

Are you tempted to toy with a relationship that isn't Christ-centered?
    Flee.
Are you tempted to buy something you can't afford?
    Flee.
Are you tempted to watch that questionable television program?
    Flee.
Are you tempted to put together a deal that isn't totally honest?
    Flee.

WHY I NEED TO KNOW ABOUT SPIRITUAL WARFARE

If spiritual warfare is a reality, and if I don't know about it and prepare for it, I stand a very good chance of becoming a casualty. I will not understand all the things that happen to me, and I will be of little value to others who are experiencing spiritual warfare.

One of the keys to winning spiritual warfare is "to know when to hold 'em and when to fold 'em." We need to fight when we should fight, flee when we should flee, and not confuse the two.

Deceiving us is not enough for this lord of death and darkness, however; for once we have sinned, he grabs the back of our heads and shoves our faces in the mud of guilt until we suffocate. By miring Christians in guilt, Satan keeps them from the joy of Christ and eliminates them as an effective force in leading others to Christ. To do this, Satan constantly accuses Christians of their sin, attempting to convince them that they have no business continuing their charade of Christian living. Of course, he does all this in the first person, so we think we are just talking to ourselves out of our own guilty conscience.

What a failure I am, what a disgusting piece of humanity, we cry. What a phony. What a pitiful excuse for a Christian. Who do I think I am, anyway? I should have known from the beginning that I couldn't make it as a moral success. I was a fool to even try. The Christian life might work for others, but it won't work for me. I'm inherently flawed. I need to give it up. Stop trying to fake it. Go back to the old life where I belong!

If we believe this father of lies, he has us right where he wants us: defeated, ineffectual, and convinced that our name brings a noxious odor to the nostrils of God.

HOW CAN WE GET THE POWER TO OVERCOME?

We are able to overcome Satan by realizing that his only power over us is that of deception and fear, and by resisting him God's way.

When I was a kid, I saw a western movie on television in which a huckster traveled from town to town with a huge rattlesnake in a glass cage. The man would cover the glass with a blanket and take it into a saloon. There he would tell the people what was under the blanket in the cage and would bet that the toughest, bravest man in town would not be able to hold his hand against the glass without jerking it back when the rattlesnake struck.

Well, the townspeople went wild with excitement. After deciding who they thought was the bravest, toughest man in town, they hurried to tell him about the bet. Of course, after having been chosen as the toughest, bravest man in town, it was impossible for the guy to resist the challenge. So he strode to the saloon, where all the folks bet that he could hold his hand against the glass without jerking it back when the rattlesnake struck.

After all bets were taken, the huckster tore the blanket off to reveal the biggest, most menacing, evil-eyed reptile ever seen by man. Annoyed by the light and noise, the snake coiled to strike, his rattles buzzing nervously.

The toughest, bravest man broke out in a cold sweat. But prodded by the collective expectation of the townspeople, he moved his hand toward the glass.

The snake coiled even tighter, the rattles buzzing their lethal warning.

Slowly the man inched his hand toward the glass and finally touched it. As he did, the snake struck with fury. And reflexively, the toughest, bravest man jerked his hand away.

A stunned silence fell over the saloon. No one could believe what had happened.

The man looked around in anguish and humiliation, then stormed from the saloon. The huckster happily collected his money and moved on to the next town to repeat the scene and, once again, win the bet. And he almost always won.

Why? Because no matter how big and brave and tough the frontiersmen were, the sight of that coiled reptile striking the nearly invisible glass was a fearsome thing. The only thing between them and certain death was a thin pane of glass. The huckster knew it would hold; the frontiersmen did not trust it. The huckster knew there was nothing to fear except fear itself, and he played on that fear to make his living.

I have often thought what a great metaphor that scenario is for spiritual warfare. The snake is Satan and the forces of evil. The glass is Jesus. For those on the safe side of the glass, for those who live a life of faith and obedience to Christ, there is nothing to fear. The only ones terrorized by the evil inside the cage are those who do not trust the glass to keep them safe, or those who stick their hands inside the glass.

> **Satan plays on our fears.**

There are two important things we must understand about spiritual warfare: first, there is real danger on the wrong side of the glass; and second, we are safe on the right side of the glass no matter how fearful things appear.

But what does that mean? Well, generally speaking, it means we must submit to God in all things and resist the devil (James 4:7). And specifically it means we must gird ourselves in the spiritual armor He has provided for us. We need

- *the belt of truth*, so that we can know, understand, believe, and obey the truth of God as revealed in the Bible and in Jesus.
- *the breastplate of righteousness*, so that we are not satisfied with known sin in our lives. We must confess any sin and, to the degree our spiritual maturity allows, live a godly lifestyle.
- *the shoes of the preparation of the gospel of peace*, so that we can rest in the truth of the promises God has given us.
- *the shield of faith* to ward off attacks of doubt, unbelief, discouragement, and temptation.
- *the helmet of salvation*, on which rests our hope in the future, and which enables us to live in this world according to the value system of the next.

- *the sword of the Spirit*, the Word of God, so that we can use the Scriptures specifically in life's situations to fend off attacks of the Enemy and put him to flight.

God doesn't want us to sin, and certainly He doesn't take our sin lightly when we do. But He is also patient and loving and gracious. And no matter what we have done, we must not be afraid to come into His presence. God's grace is sufficient for all our sins.

We are often afraid to teach this because we think people will abuse it and go out and sin like crazy. However, when people truly understand the love of God—when they understand that their relationship with Him depends not on their own ability to cleanse themselves but on His grace—the result is just the opposite.

We drop down to our knees and cry out to God in gratitude that, in spite of all our shortcomings, He does not desert us. And this profound thanksgiving and understanding of God's grace produces an increased desire to be holy.

The secret to withstanding Satan's accusations is not what we do; it is what Christ did on the cross. If we truly understand that, then once we have followed Christ's instructions for spiritual warfare, we can rest in Christ and stand against Satan's accusations.

As John White wrote in his book *The Fight*:

God's answer to your guilty conscience is the death of his Son. Your answer to a guilty conscience is usually something you do, like confessing harder, praying more, reading your Bible, paying more than your tithe in the offering and so on. Do you not understand? The Father does not welcome you because you have been trying hard, because you have made a thoroughgoing confession, or because you have been making spiritual strides recently. He does not welcome you because you have something you can be proud about. He welcomes you because his Son died for you. Are you blasphemous enough to suppose that your dead works, your feeble efforts can add to the finished work of a dying Savior? "It is finished!" he cried. Completed. Done. Forever ended. He crashed through the gates of hell, set prisoners free, abolished death and burst in new life from the tomb. All to set you free from sin and open the way for you to run into the loving arms of God.

Now do you understand how "the brethren" overcame the Accuser by the blood of the Lamb? They refused to let his accusations impede their access to God. A simple confession was enough. They face the Accuser boldly saying, "We already know the worst you could ever tell us, and so does God. What is more the blood of Jesus is enough." Therefore, when you find the grey cloud descending, whether it be as you pray, as you work, as you testify or whatever, when you find the ring of assurance going from your words because of a vague sense of guilt, look up to God and say, "Thank you, my Father, for the blood of your Son. Thank you, even now, that you accept me gladly, lovingly in spite of all I am and have done—because of his death. Father and God, I come." (87–89)

Resist the efforts of Satan to accuse you, to bury you with guilt, to make you feel worthless and unqualified to come to Christ again. Part of his warfare strategy is to make you ineffective as a witness and unhappy as a disciple. Be on guard against his wiles. Recognize them. And stand firm against him in the strength God provides.

WHAT ARE THREE PRIMARY PERSPECTIVES ON SPIRITUAL WARFARE?

The three primary perspectives on spiritual warfare are the Spiritual Resistance View, the Truth Encounter View, and the Power Encounter View.

Among those who accept spiritual warfare as a present reality for Christians, everyone agrees to a remarkable extent regarding the battlefronts of the world and the flesh. But regarding how Christians today ought to fight against the devil and his works, that agreement gives way to three basic views. First are those who believe that the believer's warfare against the devil today requires only spiritual resistance; second are those who believe that warfare must go beyond resistance to assertive truth encounter; and third are those who believe that with resistance and truth encounter, sometimes dramatic power encounters are occasionally necessary also.

A comprehensive discussion of each view is not possible in this book, but within our short space we look more closely at each view. For simplicity, for each I will mention one figure and book as representative of that view.

Spiritual Resistance View

Those who hold to the Spiritual Resistance position rely upon the New Testament books that follow the four Gospels and Acts—the Epistles—for guidance in all areas of the Christian life, including how believers should practice spiritual warfare. Because they see no examples of demon possession or of believers continuing the practice of Jesus and the disciples of casting out demons, they doubt or fully deny that such possession or exorcism, the act of casting demons out, still occurs.

The Epistles, though, in three important passages do show how believers wage spiritual warfare: by resisting or standing firm against Satan and demons:

- *Ephesians 6:11,* "Put on the full armor of God, so that you will be able to stand firm against the schemes of the devil" (NASB).

- *James 4:7*, "Submit therefore to God. Resist the devil and he will flee from you" (NASB)
- *1 Peter 5:8–9*, "Be of sober spirit, be on the alert. Your adversary, the devil, prowls about like a roaring lion, seeking someone to devour. But resist him, firm in your faith . . ."(NASB).

According to this view, at salvation we were all given everything we need to defeat our evil spiritual enemies. We ought not cast demons out of others, nor talk to demons, nor do anything else similar to performing an exorcism. Rather, we are to believe the truth and live in holiness. Then we may do as the Epistles make clear: put our armor on and stand firm—in a word, *resist*. If we resist the devil, he will flee from us. Anything else unnecessarily clouds the issue and handles the problem of demonic influence in an unbiblical way.

While he may not accept this explanation without reservation or clarification, a major proponent of this general view is John MacArthur, and his major teaching on this subject is found in his book *How to Meet the Enemy*. He believes that "truth encounter" and "power encounter" people risk relying on "technique" versus character.

MacArthur's objection to speaking to demons, binding them, and casting them out is strenuous. He argues that the authority Christ gave His disciples over demons was an ability for them only because they were His special representatives (1 Thessalonians 2:6ff; 2 Corinthians 13:10). They were privileged with this supernatural ability so that those who heard them would realize they spoke for God (2 Corinthians 12:12; Hebrews 2:3–4).

> No one today has authority over demons and disease like the apostles did. In fact, 2 Peter 2:10–11 and Jude 8–10 imply that believers are below demonic spirits on the "authority ladder," and need to implore the Lord when dealing with them.
>
> So, "taking authority" over demon spirits or negative circumstances is not a biblical concept. Our method of dealing with Satan is to resist him, firm in our faith (James 4:7, 1 Peter 5:8–9). (60)

Truth Encounter View

"Truth Encounter" is the label given by Neil Anderson, one of today's most popular writers on spiritual warfare, to his own view. Anderson believes that the authority Jesus gave His followers in Luke 9—10 is given to us also, contrary to MacArthur's view. Anderson reasons that just because the Epistles do not repeat the actual direction the Lord gave to His disciples in the Gospels does not mean that the authority is rescinded. He believes that, in fact, the Epistles actually extend to us Christ's authority over demons because we are in Christ, have been raised with Him, and are already seated with Him in the heavenly places (Ephesians 2:4–7). Since Christ continues to exert authority over demons, we who are in Him and raised with and seated with Him also have His authority now.

Anderson would certainly agree with MacArthur's emphasis on mature Christian character and the need to "resist" Satan. However, he believes that resisting the devil includes exercising authority over demons. Anderson also believes demons may attach themselves to and influence some believers in varying degrees, even to the point of a believer's being inhabited by one or more demons. He refers to this condition as demonization. (Anderson and others distinguish sharply between demonization, on the one hand, and demon possession, on the other. We discuss this distinction in the next chapter.)

In *The Bondage Breaker*, Anderson relates the story of a girl and her fiancé who came to him for counseling. Demonic influence seemed to be present, so Anderson began guiding her and her fiancé to read a prayer that was written out. At that moment, the lady let out a menacing growl, then lashed out and slapped the paper out of her fiancé's hands. Anderson spoke to the demon: "In the name of Christ and by His authority, I bind you to that chair and I command you to sit there. . . ."

Then Neil prayed, after which Janelle snapped out of a stupor. She remembered nothing that had just happened. Anderson walked her through the steps to freedom found in his book *The Bondage Breaker*. Once she had renounced involvement with sin and Satan, his hold on her was canceled (159–161).

While Anderson does take authority over demons in this manner, he does not attempt, however, to cast demons out of others.

> I have not attempted to "cast out a demon" in several years. But I have seen hundreds of people find freedom in Christ as I helped them resolve their personal and spiritual conflicts. I no longer deal directly with demons at all, and I prohibit their manifestation. I only work with their victims. As helpers, our success is dependent upon the cooperation of the persons we help. We say with Jesus to those we help, "Be it done to you according to your faith" (Matthew 9:29). Helping people understand the truth and assume personal responsibility for truth in their life is the essence of ministry. (*The Bondage Breaker,* 208)

The essence of Truth Encounter is bringing people into a personal encounter with truth, and encouraging them to respond to the truth, with the result that they are helped.

Power Encounter

Those who hold to this third position agree with the Spiritual Resistance and the Truth Encounter positions as far as they go. They believe, with the Spiritual Resistance people, that mature Christian character is the key to spiritual freedom; and they believe that people need to encounter truth to experience freedom. However, they go beyond these positions to say that some demonized believers cannot be freed without assistance from others. Therefore, they not only bind demons but also cast them out.

They base their practice on the model established by Jesus and His disciples, believing that that model is still applicable today. They reject the Spiritual Resistance view that Christians cannot be inhabited by a demon (*not* to be confused with being *possessed* by a demon). And they reject the Truth Encounter view that it is never necessary to cast out a demon. An analogy often given is that of people so physically weak and ill that they cannot recover full health alone. They need someone else to help and nurse them until they recover enough to take care of themselves. The same thing would be true spiritually, according to their understanding.

Mark Bubeck in his book *The Adversary: The Christian Versus Demon Activity* described such a power encounter between a pastor and a demon:

Pastor: "Claiming my full authority over you through my union with the Lord Jesus Christ, I command you to reveal how you were able to gain control in this person's life. I hold the blood of Christ against you and command you to tell me."

Demon: "She is afraid. We made her afraid. She's full of fear."

Pastor: "Is that the ground you claim against this child of God? Are you able to torment and work this destruction in her life because of fear?"

Demon: "Yes, she is afraid all the time, and we can work through her fear."

This conversation is reproduced as nearly as I can recall it from memory and from notes taken during an aggressive confrontation against the powers of darkness troubling a believer's life. (78)

Bubeck believes that it is a valid ministry to cast demons out of people, Christians and non-Christians. Ed Murphy, author of the comprehensive *The Handbook for Spiritual Warfare*, agrees that demons must sometimes be exorcised by a second party. He does not go looking for power encounters, but he does believe that in the course of ministering to people, situations sometimes call for a power encounter, leading to exorcism of a demon and its influence.

CONCLUSION

The Spiritual Resistance view objects to speaking to demons, binding them, and casting them out because Christ gave such authority over demons only to His special representatives, the first disciples and the apostles (1 Thessalonians 2:6ff; 2 Corinthians 13:10). They were privileged with this supernatural ability so that those who heard them would realize they spoke for God (2 Corinthians 12:12; Hebrews 2:3–4). This view further denies that a Christian can be inhabited by a demon because, as MacArthur wrote, "the indwelling of a demon evidences the absence of genuine salvation" (82).

The proponents of the Truth Encounter and Power Encounter views would certainly respect MacArthur's concern about whether people who are demonized are truly Christians. Nevertheless, their experience suggests that Christians have been demonized to the point of demonic inhabitation. In addition, they would not consider the fact that the Epistles do not describe an ongoing ministry to demonized people to count as decisive evidence against such a ministry. Yet these two Encounter views differ about exactly how such ministry is to be done.

We have then an honest difference of perspectives among intelligent, careful, well-meaning, and spiritually mature Christians. As with other areas of difference among believers, such as views about how God is sovereign and humans free moral agents or about end-times prophecy, there appear to be responsible positions that inherently conflict, and it is not possible to resolve the differences, even among earnest Christian scholars.

This situation does not mean that everyone is right, for they cannot be. But we may not know until we get to heaven what the full truth is. Perhaps as we work at trying to find as much common understanding as we can in a spirit of peace, we will find more common ground than we thought, and we can use it to foster greater unity and common cause. While we may disagree deeply on this issue, we disagree as brothers, and we ought to handle the disagreements in love, "endeavoring to keep the unity of the Spirit in the bond of peace" (Ephesians 4:3).

SPEED BUMP!

Slow down to be sure you've gotten the main points of this chapter.

Q1. What are the three battlefronts in spiritual warfare?

A1. The three battlefronts in our spiritual warfare are the world, the flesh, and the *devil.*

Q2. What is the source of our strength?

A2. The source of our strength in the spiritual war is *God* alone.

Q3. What are the weapons of war?

A3. Our weapons of war are the pieces of spiritual *armor* described in Scripture.

Q4. What are Satan's methods of deception?

A4. Satan employs two particularly effective means of deceiving us: first he gets us to sin; then, once we have sinned, he keeps us mired in *guilt.*

Q5. How can we get the power to overcome?

A5. We are able to overcome Satan by realizing that his only power over us is that of deception and fear, and by *resisting* him God's way.

Q6. What are three primary perspectives on spiritual warfare?

A6. The three primary perspectives on spiritual warfare are the Spiritual *Resistance* View, the *Truth* Encounter View, and the *Power* Encounter View.

FILL IN THE BLANK

Q1. What are the three battlefronts in spiritual warfare?

A1. The three battlefronts in our spiritual warfare are the world, the flesh, and the _____.

Q2. What is the source of our strength?

A2. The source of our strength in the spiritual war is _____ alone.

Q3. What are the weapons of war?

A3. Our weapons of war are the pieces of spiritual _____ described in Scripture.

Q4. What are Satan's methods of deception?

A4. Satan employs two particularly effective means of deceiving us: first he gets us to sin; then, once we have sinned, he keeps us mired in _____.

Q5. How can we get the power to overcome?

A5. We are able to overcome Satan by realizing that his only power over us is that of deception and fear, and by _____ him God's way.

Q6. What are three primary perspectives on spiritual warfare?

A6. The three primary perspectives on spiritual warfare are the Spiritual _____ View, the _____ Encounter View, and the _____ Encounter View.

FOR FURTHER THOUGHT AND DISCUSSION

1. Reflect on situations in your experience when you should have fought but you fled, and vice versa. What can you learn from this?

2. In what area of your life are you most susceptible to Satan's deception? What can you do to avoid being deceived?

3. In what area of life are you most tempted to try to do the work of God while ignoring the work of man?

WHAT IF I DON'T BELIEVE?

1. I deny the clear teaching of the Bible that we are in a spiritual war.

2. I will misinterpret and misunderstand many of the things that happen to me and those I love.

3. I will be soundly duped by Satan and neutralized in my spiritual walk.

4. I am likely to feel very frustrated and defeated.

5. I may be deceived to the point of my personal destruction.

FOR FURTHER STUDY

1. Scripture

Several Scripture passages speak of the reality of spiritual warfare:

- John 8:44
- Ephesians 6:11–18
- James 4:7
- Peter 5:8

Read these passages and consider how they add to your understanding of spiritual warfare.

2. Books

Several other books are very helpful in studying this subject. They are listed below according to the view they support. Read them all with care and discernment. There may be things in all of them that you don't agree with. Just because you disagree with something in one of the books does not mean it is bad. I have read all these books and found each of them helpful in coming to my own convictions regarding spiritual warfare.

1. Spiritual Resistance View:
   How to Meet the Enemy, John MacArthur
   Spiritual Warfare, Ray Stedman

2. Truth Encounter View
   The Bondage Breaker, Neil Anderson
   Victory over the Darkness, Neil Anderson

3. Power Encounter View
   The Adversary, Mark Bubeck
   The Handbook for Spiritual Warfare, Ed Murphy

2

WHO ARE THE UNSEEN FORCES IN THE INVISIBLE WAR?

In Scripture the visitation of an angel is always alarming; it has to begin by saying "Fear not." [In the arts,] the Victorian angel looks as if it were going to say, "There, there."
—C. S. Lewis

In the book *Where Angels Walk*, Joan Anderson tells about a woman who was walking alone in a dangerous section of New York when she saw a man loitering on the sidewalk ahead of her. She breathed a quick prayer and hurried past him. Later she learned that shortly afterward, another woman had been brutally attacked there.

When the first woman went to the police station, she identified in a lineup the man she had seen on the sidewalk. He turned out to be the mugger who had attacked the other woman. A policeman asked why the mugger hadn't assaulted the first woman. The man replied, "Why would I have bothered with her? She was walking down the street with two big guys, one on each side of her."

In a similar vein, the Reverend John G. Paton, a missionary in the New Hebrides Islands, told of the protective care of angels. Hostile natives surrounded his mission headquarters one night, intent on burning out the Patons and killing them. John Paton and his wife prayed all during that terror-filled night that God would deliver them. When daylight came they were amazed to see the attackers unaccountably leave.

Angels often protect the believer.

A year later, the chief of the tribe was converted to Christ, and Paton, remembering what had happened, asked the chief what had kept him and his men from burning down the house and killing them.

The chief replied in surprise, "Who were all those men you had there with you?"

"There were no men there; just my wife and I," Paton answered.

The chief argued that they had seen many men standing guard—hundreds of big men in shining garments with drawn swords in their hands. They seemed to circle the mission station, so the natives were afraid to attack. Only then did Paton realize that God had sent His angels to protect them (Billy Graham, *Angels: God's Secret Agents*, 3).

IN THIS CHAPTER WE LEARN THAT . . .

1. Angels are spirits who live mostly in an unseen realm and do the will of God.
2. Satan, probably the highest good angel before he rebelled against God, is now the enemy who opposes the will of God.
3. Demons are probably the angels who sinned by following Satan in his rebellion against God. They now oppose the will of God and do the will of Satan.

What do you do when you hear stories like the Reverend Paton's? They are so far beyond our normal experience that many of us are tempted to shake our heads in disbelief. Either Paton is a liar. Or he is deluded. Or what he said actually happened. Do you assume he is a liar? He is not known to lie. Do you accuse him of being deluded? He has shown no signs of delusion in any other area of his life. If we look at the story without a bias against him, we would assume that what he said is true unless evidence demonstrates otherwise.

Well, then, are angels for real? If they exist, what about Satan and demons? Do they exist too?

The Bible says some definite things about angels, Satan, and demons, so we go there to begin our study.

WHAT ARE GOOD ANGELS?

Angels are spirits who live mostly in an unseen realm and do the will of God.

We can make a number of observations from the Bible about angels:

- Angels were created by God to do His will (Psalms 103:20–21; 148:2–5; Colossians 1).

- They are spirit beings and usually unseen (Numbers 22:22–31; Hebrews 1:7, 13–14).
- Sometimes, however, they take on the form of a human being; when they do, we may not know they are angels just from looking at them (Genesis 19:1–5; Hebrews 13:2)
- Other times their appearance makes it plain that they are angels, not human beings (Luke 2:8–15; John 20:12).
- They never marry, and they live forever (Matthew 22:30; Luke 20:36).
- They are created higher than humans for now, but in heaven humans will be higher than angels (1 Corinthians 6:3; Hebrews 2:7).
- They have great, though sometimes limited, knowledge and power (Psalm 103:20; Isaiah 37:36; Mark 13:32; 1 Peter 1:12).
- They can stand in the very presence of God (Matthew 18:10).
- They continually worship God (Isaiah 6:3; Revelation 5:11–12).
- They care about what happens to humans and rejoice when one becomes a Christian (Luke 15:10).
- Christians likely have guardian angels (Matthew 18:10; Hebrews 1:14).
- There are countless numbers of angels (Revelation 5:11).

We can also make a number of observations from the Bible about what angels do:

- Angels do whatever God wants them to do (Psalm 103:20–21).
- They punish those who rebel against God (1 Chronicles 21:15; Acts 12:23).
- Angels often took care of, defended, and protected God's people when it was His will that they do so (1 Kings 19:5; Daniel 6:22; Acts 5:19; 12:8–11).
- They may guide Christians to witness to certain unbelievers (Acts 8:26).
- They will come with Christ when He returns to earth (Matthew 25:31).
- They are organized in a hierarchy of power (Daniel 10:13, 21; Matthew 26:53; Colossians 1:16; Jude 9).
- Angels are somehow interested in and connected to the church today (1 Timothy 5:21; 1 Peter 1:12).
- Michael, a high and powerful angel, appears to be a warring angel (Daniel 10:13, 21; Jude 9; Revelation 12:7).
- Gabriel, also a high and powerful angel, appears primarily to be a messenger. He explained a vision to Daniel in the Old Testament and announced the two great births of the New Testament, those of John the Baptist and Jesus (Daniel 8:16; Luke 1:19, 26–33).

In much popular art, angels have wings and often look feminine with blond hair and blue eyes. Sometimes they appear as chubby babies. The Bible doesn't support this imagery. Angels in the Bible usually appear in human form. In Isaiah 6 and Revelation 4:5, the angels attending God's throne have three pairs of wings, not the one pair normally depicted. Some people think that humans become angels when they die and go to heaven. From what we have already learned about angels, this cannot be possible.

WHO IS SATAN?

Satan, probably the highest good angel before he rebelled against
God, is now the enemy who opposes the will of God.

Throughout the years, it has been considered unsophisticated to believe in Satan. How could a person take seriously a being that runs around in red underwear with a tail, cloven hooves, and horns growing out of his head? This picture of Satan lacks biblical foundation, however, and the number of people who believe in a literal evil being called Satan is rising meteorically. At the same time, more and more people are involving themselves in witchcraft, the occult, and satanism in the United States and around the world.

We can make a number of observations from the Bible about Satan:

- The name *Satan* means adversary or enemy. The apostle Peter even calls him "your adversary the devil" (1 Peter 5:8).
- Originally called Lucifer, which means Day Star (Isaiah 14:12), Satan is a spirit being and was possibly the highest angel in God's created order (Ezekiel 28:14–15; Luke 10:18–20).
- He sinned by rebelling against God, however, and became the ultimate evil being in the universe, the enemy who opposes God's will.
- His sin was pride. He wanted to be like God, not in the sense of possessing God's holy character, but by possessing authority equal to God's (Isaiah 14:13–15; 1 Timothy 3:6).
- His goal is to set up his own kingdom and rule in place of God (Isaiah 14:13–14; Matthew 4:8–9).
- Satan is the arch deceiver and destroyer. Jesus even called him a murderer, a liar, and the father of all lies (John 8:44; Revelation 9:11; 12:9; 20:10).
- Satan aims to destroy us. He blinds the minds of unbelievers so that they might not believe the gospel. The ruler over all the demons, he employs them to try

to defeat us, and he tempts us to sin (Matthew 12:24–27; 1 Corinthians 7:5; 2 Corinthians 4:4; Ephesians 6:11–12).

- Extremely powerful, Satan is the god of this age and the prince of the power of the air (2 Corinthians 4:4; Ephesians 2:2).
- Satan is not all-knowing and not able to be more than one place at a time. While very powerful, his power is limited. His intelligence and his army of demons who carry out his orders make him seem more powerful than he is (Job 1:7–12; 2:4–6).
- Satan (and presumably his demons) disguises himself as an angel of light to deceive people into thinking that he and his demons are good spirits, when in fact they are evil (2 Corinthians 11:13–15).
- In the end, Jesus will triumph over Satan, who will be eternally judged for his unspeakable evil (Revelation 20:10).

WHAT ARE DEMONS?

Demons are probably the angels who sinned by following Satan in his rebellion against God. They now oppose the will of God and do the will of Satan.

The Bible also informs us about the character and work of demons:

- Demons are spirit beings, probably the angels who followed Satan's rebellion against God and joined him in opposing the will of God (Luke 10:17–20; Revelation 12:7–9).
- Demons seem to be organized into an army-like hierarchy, with some seeming to be the spiritual power behind kingdoms, nations, and governments, while others focus on individuals (Daniel 10:13; Isaiah 14:12; Ezekiel 28:13–19; Ephesians 6:12).
- They have their own "doctrine," which they promote among humans to deceive and destroy them (1 Timothy 4:1–3).
- Demons can exert various degrees of control over individuals, inflict physical maladies, cause insanity or derangement, give a person extraordinary strength and seemingly supernatural abilities, and take over a person's life and destiny if allowed (Matthew 9:32–33; 10:8; 17:15–18; Mark 6:13; Luke 8:26–31; Acts 16:16–24).

A major question that must be answered is whether or not people today can be demon possessed. Some believe it is possible since various translations of the Bible, following the lead of the King James Bible, refer to demon possession (see Matthew 8:16 as an example).

However, there are three difficulties with such translations. First, the words *demon possessed* and *demon possession* do not occur in the original language (Greek) of the New Testament. Our English word *demon* was brought directly into English (transliterated) from the Greek word *daimon.* The verb form of *daimon,* which is *dai-monizomai,* is commonly translated "demon possessed," but it would be better simply to bring it into the English as "demonize."

WHY I NEED TO KNOW THIS

I must know about both good and evil spirits in order to be blessed and encouraged by the good, and to be protected from and victorious over the evil.

Second, because the words *demon possessed* do not occur in the original language, we cannot say for sure what it might be to be demon possessed. While "to be demonized" is never defined, we have descriptions of instances of demonic influence in Scripture that vary in intensity. On the extreme end, we read of the Gadarene demoniac who sadistically cut himself, wore no clothes, lived among the tombs, and appeared to be under the continuous control of demons (Mark 5:1–15). On a lesser scale, we read of Peter trying to persuade Jesus not to submit to crucifixion, and Jesus said, "Get behind Me, Satan" (Matthew 16:23).

Third, to speak of "demon possession" encourages an erroneous "all-or-nothing" concept of demonic influence in a person's life. It can easily be misunderstood that either a person is free of demonic influence or he is demon possessed. However, that observation is not warranted by the original language of the Bible, by the examples in the Bible, or from observing those who have witnessed or experienced demonic influence.

To use the word *demonize* allows us, rightly, to speak of demonic influence without necessarily defining how much influence. A person might be mildly demonized or severely demonized. This term is more accurate and more helpful than being limited to the options of "possessed" or " not possessed."

We might define being "demonized" as being under the influence of one or more demons. This definition allows for Christians as well as non-Christians to be demonized and for degrees of demonization from mild to severe. The more extreme forms of demonization in the Bible seem to include a demon actually inhabiting the body of a person. We read of people having a demon and asking Jesus to cast the demon out of a loved one. Jesus does, and the demon(s) leave (Mark 7:26).

Those who prefer the term "demon possession," are usually referring to the *inhabiting* of a human by one or more demons. If someone is being *influenced* by a demon, but not actually inhabited, they would usually refer to that as being "demon oppressed." Yet no consensus exists among those who use these terms as to whether a *Christian* can be "demon possessed." Since no translation of the Bible refers to demonization after the book of Acts, some conclude that demon possession does not occur after Acts. Others that it may occur with non-Christians, but not with Christians.

Those who prefer the term "demonization" over "demon possession" believe that silence on the subject after the book of Acts does not necessarily mean that demonization no longer occurs. Cessation of all demonic influence like that recorded in the Gospels and Acts is a possible conclusion, but the silence of the Epistles about demonization could also be a coincidence. Or their silence might be the result of different purposes and forms of writing that the Epistles manifest compared to the Gospels and Acts. As letters responding to specific and general problems within the earliest Christian churches, the Epistles do not emphasize descriptions of action, while books of historical narrative such as the Gospels and Acts consist primarily of described action. Perhaps then an absolute conclusion from the biblical text alone is not possible. Yet many people have observed activity that appears to be very similar to the demonic activity in the Gospels and book of Acts. Their observations suggest that demonization still occurs today.

CONCLUSION

"God, show yourself stronger than the spirits!"

For years, Joanne Shetler, Wycliff missionary to a remote and primitive people in the Philippines, had prayed that prayer. For centuries, the Balangao people had worshiped the capricious and hard-to-please spirits who made relentless demands for sacrifices. The Balangao knew the spirits had power.

Now, some of the villagers who were beginning to take Shetler seriously were causing an uproar throughout the whole village. Two old women who had been powerful spirit mediums had decided to worship God. The angered spirits terrorized the village. The terrified people pleaded with Joanne not to allow the women to worship God lest the spirits kill the former mediums. In the past those who had tried to quit serving the spirits had paid with their lives, so everyone was watching, waiting for the two former spirit mediums to die.

When the two old women didn't die, these primitive people opened themselves to the Scripture. The Balangao learned that God had power greater than that of the demonic spirits they had formerly served. Shetler recorded these and many other dramatic events in her book *And the Word Came with Power.*

This is only one story. Countless others also tell of direct encounters with forces of darkness. To the many people who never come into contact with anything remotely close to overt demonic demonstrations, the stories that others tell seem simply too fantastic to believe. I used to be one of those people. But those who have crossed paths with the dark side have no difficulty believing them.

Although there is no connection between them, both the New Age movement, on the one hand, and the charismatic and Third Wave movements, on the other, have raised an interest in angels. One danger emerging from this increased interest is that people have seemingly benign experiences with what they think are angels when they are probably evil demons. The angels in many of the newly appearing stories don't resemble the angels in Scripture. Numerous current stories describe angels that materialize on command to help a person in trouble, almost like genies. These angels do not confront anyone with sin and never demand changes in a person's behavior or character.

In the Bible, however, when an angel appeared undisguised and spoke, its first words were usually, "Fear not." I doubt that angels waste words. My guess is that angels say this because the people who see them as *angels* and not as humans are terrified, initially. Angels are awesome, powerful beings who deliver messages from God that often include moral judgment on actions and attitudes. They are not genies let out of a bottle, to grant us three wishes. Messengers from God, they represent God to us.

Angels and demons do exist. Angels may very well have slipped in and out of events in your life without your ever knowing it. They may have been invisible or they may have taken on a human form so that you would never know an angel had visited you. And although demonic forces are to be taken very seriously, the Christian need not fear them, for "greater is He who is in you than he who is in the world" (1 John 4:4 NASB). The powers of darkness encompass a hierarchy of evil spiritual beings who do the bidding of their master, Satan. The powers of light comprise a hierarchy of good angels who do the bidding of their Master, God. Difficult though it is for us to think in these terms, we must become aware of the invisible world that surrounds us: forces of darkness locked in mortal combat with the forces of light. Spiritual warfare is a reality!

SPEED BUMP!

Slow down to be sure you've gotten the main points of this chapter.

Q1. What are good angels?

A1. Angels are *spirits* who live mostly in an unseen realm and do the will of God.

Q2. Who is Satan?

A2. Satan, probably the highest good angel before he rebelled against God, is now the *enemy* who opposes the will of God.

Q3. What are demons?

A3. Demons are probably the angels who *sinned* by following Satan in his rebellion against God. They now oppose the will of God and do the will of Satan.

FILL IN THE BLANK

Q1. What are good angels?

A1. Angels are _____ who live mostly in an unseen realm and do the will of God.

Q2. Who is Satan?

A2. Satan, probably the highest good angel before he rebelled against God, is now the _____ who opposes the will of God.

Q3. What are demons?

A3. Demons are probably the angels who _____ by following Satan in his rebellion against God. They now oppose the will of God and do the will of Satan.

FURTHER THOUGHT AND DISCUSSION

1. Have you ever had an experience in which you were saved from disaster so dramatically that you suspect an angel might have saved you?

2. Have you ever had an encounter with a person who was so unusual that you suspect it was an angel disguised in a human form?

3. Have you ever had an encounter with evil that was so vivid that you suspect a demon was involved?

4. Do you believe that you understand spiritual warfare well enough to be safe? As you read the rest of this book, what answers do you hope you will receive to your questions about spiritual warfare?

WHAT IF I DON'T BELIEVE?

1. If I don't know that angels exist, I may misunderstand, misinterpret, or miss altogether, the work of an angel in my life. I would lose the confidence of knowing that there is probably an angel assigned to every Christian, and that nothing can happen to me God does not allow.

2. If I do not believe in Satan, I will not be alert to his attempts to deceive and destroy me. I could easily become a hapless victim simply because of my ignorance or unbelief.

3. If I do not believe in demons, not only will I be susceptible to their deviousness, but also, I could get drawn into evil, not understanding or believing how to be victorious against them.

4. I need to know what characterizes both good angels and demons and what actions are typical of each, so that I will not be deceived into thinking that actions of demons are actually those of angels.

FOR FURTHER STUDY

1. Scripture

Several key passages in the Bible speak of angels, demons, and Satan. Many references have been given in this chapter already. However, some of the key passages are highlighted below.

- Isaiah 6:1–8
- 2 Corinthians 11:14
- Ephesians 2:2
- Ephesians 6:10–13
- Hebrews 1:14
- Hebrews 13:2
- James 4:7
- 1 Peter 5:8
- Jude 6
- Revelation 4–5

2. Books

Several other books are very helpful in studying this subject further. They are listed below.

Know What You Believe, Paul Little

Angels: God's Secret Messengers, Billy Graham

Spiritual Warfare, Ray Stedman

3

WHAT IS THE BELT OF TRUTH?

Nobody can tell bigger "lies" than fishermen. Exaggerating the size of the fish they "almost caught" or of "the one that got away" has given us the term *fish story.* In fact, one fishing contest holds a lying contest afterward. The person who catches the biggest fish gets an award, but so does the person who tells the biggest fish story, and often the size of the fish pales in comparison with the size of the story. One contestant said that he had found a place where the fishing was so good that he had to stand behind a tree to bait his hook. Once when he wasn't paying close attention and forgot to stand behind the tree, a seven-pound largemouth bass jumped out of the lake, cleared thirty feet of shore, and bit the hook while the fisherman was still baiting it.

When it comes to promoting tall tales, Burlington, Wisconsin, boasts a Liar's Club, which anyone can join for one dollar and a good enough lie, and many whoppers have been submitted over the years. One aspiring member told of fog so thick when they cut down a tree, it didn't fall over until the fog lifted. Another said his wife was so lazy that she fed the chickens popcorn so the eggs would turn themselves over when she fried them. Last year it was so dry, another claimed, that the bullfrogs born in the spring never learned how to swim. And one man said his wife's feet were so cold that every time she took off her shoes, the furnace kicked on.

Everyone knows and understands, of course, that this isn't really lying. This "tall-telling" is really just a form of entertainment. So we all laugh or smile, but never take it seriously.

Part of the American ethic is that you tell the truth. Even those who lie believe that "truth" ought to be part of the American ethic. From the earliest days when we heard the story of George Washington admitting that he could not tell a lie, he did cut down the cherry tree, to our national outrage at President Nixon's duplicity over the Watergate scandal, we believe that good Americans tell the truth.

Yet in "A Nation of Liars?" commentator Merrill McLoughlin observes that

scandal is rocking the government, and voters have come off elections in which they were deluged with negative advertisement, much of it ridden with misleading innuendo. Wall Street is still reeling from revelations of unscrupulous business practices. There has been a rash of revelations about hyped and falsified scientific research: A study published last month accused forty-seven scientists at the Harvard and Emory University medical schools of producing misleading papers. A House subcommittee estimated last year that one out of every three working Americans is hired with educational or career credentials that have been altered in some way. (*US News & World Report*, Feb. 23, 1987: 54)

The alarming impression here is that America is growing dishonest. While people think everyone else ought to tell the truth, more and more people feel free to lie when it suits their purpose. Lying, both in personal and public life, is much more common than it used to be.

Americans seem to be growing increasingly dishonest.

A Grand Canyon of differences separates harmless tall tales and the plague of lies insidiously infecting our society. Nothing points up more clearly the need for the truth than McLoughlin's article. And no one needs to be more aware of the truth than Christians, who must be committed to learning the truth and living it in actions and words. About truth, the Bible is unequivocal. Truth is the first weapon in the believer's arsenal—the first piece in the full armor of God.

In preparing to do battle with the evil mastermind and his unholy hosts who are out to deceive and destroy us, we must acknowledge and follow certain spiritual truths if we are to be victors. To vividly communicate these spiritual truths, the apostle Paul used the imagery of the armor of a Roman soldier. There are six pieces of armor, Paul said, and if we wear them— adhere to these truths—we can win spiritual battles.

WHAT DOES THE BELT OF TRUTH PICTURE?

The belt of truth pictures a commitment to the truth of the Word of God.

"Stand therefore, having girded your waist with truth . . . (Ephesians 6:14).

The first piece of spiritual armor is the belt of truth. The Roman soldier wore a thick leather belt to hold his tunic in place and to which was attached the sheath for his sword. When the Roman soldier "girded his loins" he tucked his long outer robe under his belt so that it would not hinder him in running or fighting.

In similar fashion, the Christian must prepare himself for spiritual battle by fixing in place his commitment to the truth of Scripture, and setting his mind to follow that truth. This prevents folds of falsehood from entangling his legs and tripping him, making him vulnerable in battle.

Peter used the same imagery in 1 Peter 1:13 when he wrote: "Therefore, gird up the loins of your mind, be sober, and rest your hope fully upon the grace that is to be brought to you at the revelation of Jesus Christ." This means, "Prepare your minds for action. Get ready for combat. Be self-controlled. Get focused."

The Christian must prepare himself for battle by making a total commitment to the truth of Scripture and by being determined to follow that truth.

WHAT MUST OUR LEVEL OF COMMITMENT TO TRUTH BE?

Our commitment to truth must be total and unending.

Semper Fidelis (Always Faithful) is the official, etched-in-stone motto of the U.S. Marine Corps. Since 1775, marines have been the first to fight in almost every major war of the United States. For over two hundred years, "from the halls of Montezuma to the shores of Tripoli," the marines have stood for loyalty, discipline, and faithfulness.

Imagine the damage done to that image, then, when in a 1987 "spy-secrets for sex" scandal two marine guards at the U.S. embassy in Moscow escorted Soviet agents into the most sensitive chambers of the consulate, including the "secure" communications center. The damage? Incalculable. It threatened entire lists of secret agents, compromised transmission codes, and immobilized carefully designed plans.

Truth has great significance in our lives. Individual truth or falsehood affects everyone around us. Without a basic level of morality, without a foundation of trust and dependability, society breaks down. Business cannot be conducted without spending billions of dollars on legal fees to protect us from those who would take advantage of us. Billions of dollars of tax money must go to build prisons and house and feed prisoners. School systems crumble, families fall apart, welfare and social aid collapse. In short, society disintegrates.

Unless people are fundamentally true to their word, democracy cannot function. The more that people depart from truth, the more national problems develop and the more society disintegrates.

"Do not be deceived," Paul wrote to the Galatians, "God is not mocked; for whatever a man sows, that he will also reap" (Galatians 6:7). If we sow lies and dishonesty, we will reap corruption and disintegration. It is a philosophical and political necessity to be true to our word.

But the believer's commitment to truth goes far beyond a philosophical understanding of the importance of truth in society. We must be committed to truth ourselves—committed to believing the truth and to living it.

There is the truth (as in "telling the truth") and there is Truth. God is Truth. He is always true to what is and true to His word. He always and only speaks and acts that which is true. And since we are created to be like God, we must speak and act according to what is true.

IN THIS CHAPTER WE LEARN THAT . . .

1. The belt of truth pictures a commitment to the truth of the Word of God.

2. Our commitment to truth must be total and unending.

3. The Christian must tell the truth in word and deed, or else his character, the credibility of the gospel, and the reputation of God Himself are compromised.

4. God's truth is absolute, eternal, and unchanging.

Can you imagine God not being true to His word: "Oh, yes, I know I said I would break into history and put an end to sin and pain and unrighteousness and set up a new heaven and a new earth where My children would live forever in love and joy and peace, but I lied"? Can you imagine God saying, "Calvary was a joke, a hoax. Your sins aren't forgiven after all. You'll have to make it on your own. Good luck"?

It is incomprehensible, isn't it? And a truly fearsome thought. We count on God to be true to every aspect of His word. As God is true to His word, we are to be like Him and must be true to our word. This means that

- we must embrace the total truth of Scripture;
- we must speak the truth and be true to our word;
- we must back up what we say by how we live.

When we are committed to believing the truth, we believe the promises of God and rest in them; we believe the commands of God and obey them; and we trust the truth of Scripture and order our lives according to it.

This is what it means to buckle on the belt of truth.

WHY MUST A CHRISTIAN TELL THE TRUTH IN WORD AND IN DEED?

The Christian must tell the truth in word and deed, or else his character, the credibility of the gospel, and the reputation of God Himself are compromised.

"When we can no longer depend on one another to do what we said we would do, the future becomes an undefined nightmare," said Ted Engstrom in his book *Integrity*. "What about our lawmakers? Do they obey their own laws? Have our preachers heard their own sermons on repentance? Is the business world sold on ethics? Are 'lovers' truly loving one another? Are parents producing character in their children or just raising characters?" (3–4).

It seems not.

The results of a recent Gallup poll revealed that the ethical standards of Christians in the workplace were no higher than those of non-Christians. This included being honest about business facts and being true to one's word. This is alarming news! If anyone should stand apart from the crowd in the matter of truthfulness, it should be the Christian!

Now, I know that this issue is not an easy or a simple one. For centuries theologians and philosophers have debated whether or not it is ever proper to tell a lie. For example, is it all right to tell a lie to save a life—as Rahab did, in the time of Joshua, to save the lives of the Israelite spies? Or, as Winston Churchill once said, "In wartime, truth is so precious that she should be attended by a bodyguard of lies."

My purpose is not to get into theoretical extremes, but to call the church to higher ground. We must step up to higher morals and ethics—in how we work, how we treat others, and how we act—founded on our commitment to Christ. We must not be carriers of the "lie" disease that is infecting our society, for God hates lying.

"You shall not bear false witness against your neighbor," says the ninth commandment (Exodus 20:16). "These six things the LORD hates," says Proverbs, and one of them is "a lying tongue" (Proverbs 6:16–17). "Therefore," wrote Paul, "laying aside falsehood, speak truth" (Ephesians 4:25 NASB).

The moral disintegration in society, while a terrible thing, does present an opportunity to face people with the truth of Christ and the Bible. And since they have no answers for the dilemmas we face on every front, more and more people are willing to listen.

We must, therefore, be committed to the truth in word and deed. We must be people of the truth, not people of the lie. We must be people of integrity.

The word *integrity* comes from the root word *integer*, which means "whole." Often used in mathematics, an integer is a whole number. To be a person of integrity has come to mean being an honest and ethical person, but this evolved from the idea of being a whole person.

WHY I NEED TO KNOW THIS

If I am not committed to learning the truth and telling it, I fall into a web of deceit and self-deceit that can only mean trouble at best and ruin at worst.

To be a whole person, there must be consistency between what we say and what we do. We cannot be duplicitous, two-sided, hypocritical; we cannot say one thing and do another. If we are people of integrity, our lives back up what we say. Thus if we say that evangelism is important but are not engaged in evangelism, we are not yet whole. We are not yet integrated. It means that if we say that supporting Christian ministries is important but we don't give generously, we are not yet integrated. If we say that our families are important but do nothing to build them, we are not yet integrated. A person of integrity puts his life where his mouth is.

We are not teaching perfectionism, of course. We will all stumble and fall at times in our pursuit of truth. God knows that. That's why He sent Jesus to die for our sin. At times the belt of truth may loosen and slide around a bit. But we can always cinch it tighter when that happens.

Whenever we function on anything that is not true, we place ourselves in jeopardy. Things are not true because the Bible says they are; the Bible says they are true because they are.

IS TRUTH ABSOLUTE OR RELATIVE?

God's truth is absolute, eternal, and unchanging.

Relativism is the belief that all truth is relative. Alan Bloom, in his master work *The Closing of the American Mind*, states that the single most agreed-upon "truth" in America today is that truth is relative. There is no such thing as absolute truth. Each person is free to determine truth for himself. You may believe one thing, and I believe the opposite, but that is okay because each thing is true for the one who believes it.

This perspective is wreaking havoc with business, our education system, our government, the family, morals and values, the church, and everything else in American life, because as a result, "everyone did what was right in his own eyes" (Judges 21:25). When everyone does what is right in his own eyes, a democracy, which depends on cooperative action, begins to break down. And to the degree that this affects the church (and whatever affects society always affects the church), the church begins to lose its ability to impact society.

That is why our society is disintegrating from within, that is why the church seems so powerless to influence society, and that is why lives, even Christians ones, are often in upheaval and disarray. We are paying the price culturally, ecclesiastically, and personally, of living in a society that has abandoned absolute truth.

When people wonder what is wrong with America, the answer is, as Alexander Solzhenitsyn said, "Men have forgotten God." And with the forgetting of God comes the loss of absolute truth, and with the loss of absolute truth everything disintegrates.

But not only do we pay a dreadful price as an American culture, we as individual Christians and the church as a whole also pay a dreadful price. When we Christians abandon absolute truth in favor of relativism, we destroy the integrity of the Bible, since it claims to be "absolute truth"; we lose a keen sense of sin, since each person becomes free to determine for himself what is right and wrong; we forfeit a righteous culture within the church, and thus our testimony to those outside; we sacrifice the ability to explain the universe and humanity, since the Bible tells us their origin and nature.

> **Disintegration follows loss of absolute truth.**

CONCLUSION

James Boice, pastor of the venerable Tenth Presbyterian Church in Philadelphia, has written:

> In ancient times . . . the finest pottery was thin. It had a clear color, and it brought a high price. Fine pottery was very fragile both before and after firing. And . . . this pottery would sometimes crack in the oven. Cracked pottery should have been thrown away. But dishonest dealers were in the habit of filling in the cracks with a hard pearl wax that would blend in with the color of the pottery. This made the cracks practically undetectable in the shops, especially when painted or glazed; but the wax was immediately detectable if the pottery was held up to light, especially to the sun. In that case the cracks would show up darker. It was said that the artificial element was

detected by "sun-testing." Honest dealers marked their finer product by the caption *sine cera*—"without wax." *(Philippians: An Expositional Commentary*, 55)

The light of the sun revealed defects. In the same way, the light of truth reveals error. Without the light of the sun, unwitting buyers would be victimized by unscrupulous merchandisers and would lose their money through the purchase of a defective product. Without the light of the Scripture, without the light of the truth, we would all be deluded by the treacherous forces of darkness trying to con us into buying an inferior product—error—instead of the genuine thing—truth. Without truth, our lives would disintegrate into shambles.

Truth and a love for truth are important because Satan is a liar and the father of lies (John 8:44). One of his primary goals is to twist the truth, to conceal the truth, to tell half-truths that act as lies, and to deceive us into believing something false. He is a deceiver and a destroyer. He deceives in order to destroy. We must therefore know the truth, be committed to the truth, live the truth, and declare the truth. Truth is the only way to victory in the spiritual war. We must buckle on the belt of truth.

SPEED BUMP!

Slow down long enough to be sure you've gotten the main points of this chapter.

Q1. What does the belt of truth picture?

A1. The belt of truth pictures a *commitment* to the truth of the Word of God.

Q2. What must our level of commitment to truth be?

A2. Our commitment to truth must be *total* and unending.

Q3. Why must a Christian tell the truth in word and in deed?

A3. The Christian must tell the truth in word and deed, or else his character, the *credibility* of the gospel, and the reputation of God, Himself, are compromised.

Q4. Is truth absolute or relative?

A4. God's truth is *absolute*, eternal, and unchanging.

FILL IN THE BLANK

Q1. What does the belt of truth picture?

A1. The belt of truth pictures a _____ to the truth of the Word of God.

Q2. What must our level of commitment to truth be?

A2. Our commitment to truth must be _____ and unending.

Q3. Why must a Christian tell the truth in word and in deed?

A3. The Christian must tell the truth in word and deed, or else his character, the _____ of the gospel, and the reputation of God, Himself, are compromised.

Q4. Is truth absolute or relative?

A4. God's truth is _____, eternal, and unchanging.

FOR FURTHER THOUGHT AND DISCUSSION

1. What are some of the greatest problems that have been created because people have failed to be true to their word (these may be in the personal, political, social, or other arenas of life)?

2. What problems might arise for a person who decided to always tell the truth?

3. What evidence do you see in your own life that you have put on the belt of truth? Is there any evidence that you may have let it slip a little? Explain.

WHAT IF I DON'T BELIEVE?

1. If I don't believe in the absolute truth of Scripture, I cast myself adrift on a sea of uncertainty, incapable of knowing anything for sure, and without any basis for hope.

2. If I don't commit myself to truth, I expose myself to damaging consequences when I violate truth.

3. If I claim to be a Christian but don't live my life according to the truth, I tarnish my own reputation as well as the reputation of the Gospel and God Himself.

FOR FURTHER STUDY

1. Scripture

Several Scripture passages speak of the importance of truth:

- John 8:32
- Romans 1:25
- Ephesians 6:14
- 2 Timothy 2:15
- 1 Peter 1:22

Read these passages and consider how they add to your understanding of the importance of truth.

2. Books

Several other books are very helpful in studying this subject. They are listed below in general order of difficulty.

30 Days to Understanding How to Live as a Christian, Max Anders

The Bible: Embracing God's Truth, Max Anders

The Lies We Believe, Chris Thurman

4

Holiness is not a series of do's and don'ts, but a conformity to God's character in the very depths of our being. This conformity is possible only as we are united with Christ.
—**Jerry Bridges**

WHAT IS THE BREASTPLATE OF RIGHTEOUSNESS?

Gary Richmond, a zookeeper at the Los Angeles Zoo, was given master keys to every animal's cage. He was cautioned sternly to guard them with his life and to pay exacting attention to which doors he opened and which doors he closed.

"Richmond," the supervisor said, "these keys will let you in to care for millions of dollars worth of animals. Some of them could never be replaced, but you could be, if you catch my drift. Some of the animals would hurt themselves if they got out, and more significantly, they might hurt and even kill somebody. You wouldn't want that on your conscience."

I took him seriously, and performed flawlessly for four months. Then, something happened with the most dangerous animal at the zoo. Ivan was a polar bear who weighed well over nine hundred pounds and had killed two prospective mates. He hated people and never missed an opportunity to attempt to grab anyone passing by his cage.

I let him out of his night quarters into the sparkling morning sunshine by pulling a lever to his guillotine door. No sooner had he passed under it than I realized that, at the other end of the hall, I had left another door opened. It was the door I would use to go outside if Ivan was locked up inside. Now Ivan could walk to the other end of the outdoor exhibit and come in that door I had left open, and, if he so chose, eat me.

In terror, I looked out the guillotine door. Ivan was still in sight. He was a creature of routine, and he always spent the first hour of his morning pacing. His pattern was L-shaped. He would walk from the door five steps straight out, and then rum right for three steps. He would then rock back and forth and come back to the guillotine door again, which he would bump with his head. He would repeat that cycle for one hour and then rest.

I timed his cycle and determined that I had seventeen seconds to run down the hallway and shut the open door. I staked my life on the fact that he would not vary his routine. He didn't seem to notice the wide open door, which is unusual. Animals tend to notice the slightest changes in their environment.

I decided that when he made his next turn, I would run down the hallway, hoping upon hope that I would not meet Ivan at the other end.

IN THIS CHAPTER WE LEARN THAT . . .

1. The breastplate of righteousness pictures a lifestyle of trusting obedience to God.

2. Righteousness is both imputed and imparted.

3. We don the breastplate of daily righteous living by being faithfully obedient to all we understand Christ is asking of us.

4. Sin hurts us by inflicting predictably painful consequences.

He turned and I ran. With every step my knees weakened. My heart pounded so hard I felt sure it would burst from fear. I made the corner and faced the critical moment. Ivan was still out of sight; I lunged for the door handle. As I reached out for the handle, I looked to the right. There was the bear . . . eight feet away. Our eyes met. His were cold and unfeeling . . . and I'm sure mine expressed all the terror that filled the moment. I pulled the huge steel door with all my strength. It clanged shut and the clasp was secured. My knees buckled and I fell to the floor racked with the effects of too much adrenaline. I looked up and Ivan was staring at me through the window in the door. (*A View from the Zoo*, 25–27. Used by permission)

"Take care of these keys," the supervisor had instructed Richmond. "Guard them carefully. Pay strict attention to which doors you open and which doors you close." He held up a standard and exhorted the zookeeper, in gravest terms, not to fall short of that standard.

Why was that? Because he was a fussbudget? A worrywart? Because he wanted to limit his employee's freedom or stifle his enjoyment of life?

No, he held up a standard for Richmond to adhere to in order to protect Richmond, the animals, and all the visitors in the zoo. Love, care, and concern set the standard, not a narrow, restrictive outlook.

So it is with God. He sets standards for us and exhorts us to adhere to them, not because He is a cosmic killjoy, a celestial fussbudget, or a heavenly worrywart, but because he sees reality clearly. He knows about consequences and cause-and-effect relationships. And He has built into His created order the necessary restrictions to keep us from harming ourselves and others.

Part of the reality He sees is spiritual warfare. He knows that our foes are not flesh and blood, but the powers of darkness, the "spiritual hosts of wickedness" (Ephesians 6:12).

We don't see or hear them. We can't touch, taste, or smell them. But they are here. This evil empire does the bidding of Satan, and its goal is to deceive and destroy those who follow God. And if it cannot destroy us, it at least wants to neutralize us so that we will not be of any consequence in leading others to follow Christ.

> **Righteousness is God's way of protecting us.**

If we want to be effective in this spiritual battle, Paul tells us, we must put on certain pieces of spiritual armor. One piece of that armor is the breastplate of righteousness.

WHAT DOES THE BREASTPLATE OF RIGHTEOUSNESS PICTURE?

The breastplate of righteousness pictures a lifestyle of trusting obedience to God.

Stand therefore . . . having put on the breastplate of righteousness (Ephesians 6:14).

The breastplate was an important part of the Roman soldier's battle gear. A metal cast of a human torso, it protected the upper part of his body, including his heart and lungs, from the arrows and spears of the enemy.

Using the analogy between literal armor and spiritual armor, we would say that the spiritual breastplate—the breastplate of righteousness—is for our protection. It is defensive armor that protects us in three ways.

1. Righteousness protects us from the harm and damage and violent ravages of sin.

2. Righteousness guards us from the hardening and choking of the spiritual arteries that suffocate the spiritual life more slowly and less violently than overt sins, but which render us lifeless, nevertheless. It keeps us from drifting away from God and dying a slow, cold death.

3. Righteousness defends us against Satan's deceptive methods by giving us discernment.

Righteousness arms us against sexual promiscuity and as a result protects us from venereal disease, AIDS, and other deadly consequences. Righteousness fortifies us against drugs and other addictions that can destroy our minds and our bodies.

Righteousness shields us from the dishonesty that can result in economic, social, and personal catastrophe and even prison. Righteousness protects us from the consequences of sin.

There is a tax on sin that we must always pay; there is no tax evasion in the spiritual realm. Sometimes sooner, sometimes later, we always pay. The breastplate of righteousness is God's divine protection against the violent ravages of sin.

God demands that we live righteously because He loves us and wants the best for us.

WHAT ARE THE TWO DIMENSIONS OF RIGHTEOUSNESS?

Righteousness is both imputed and imparted.

Imputed Righteousness

Actually, righteousness has two layers to it. The first layer is the righteousness imputed to us, which refers to Christ's righteousness that was applied to our heavenly account when we became Christians. Imputed righteousness was affixed to us as a breastplate at the moment of salvation. It is a gift from God. On the basis of Christ's work in our behalf we have been made righteous—fit for heaven, acceptable to God. We are covered, protected with the breastplate of righteousness.

As Christians, God has given us power over Satan and his hosts. We have Jesus living in us. We have the Holy Spirit living in us. The Bible says, "He who is in you is greater than he who is in the world" (1 John 4:4).

So part of the daily spiritual warfare is realizing that we are God's children. Christ's righteousness has been imputed to our account. When Satan accuses us and condemns us, telling us we have no business trying to be a Christian, when he hisses at us that we are no good and tries to bury us with guilt because we are not perfect— remember, it is all a lie from the father of lies. We don't get to heaven by being good. We don't get to be a child of God by being good. We get to be a child of God by being born again into His spiritual family, and that happens by believing in Jesus and committing our lives to Him.

We are on one side of the glass. Satan is on the other side, preparing to strike. Christ is the glass in the middle, protecting us. We must trust the glass . . . we must trust the breastplate of righteousness. Satan has nothing that can hurt us except his lies. Count on your imputed righteousness. It is important in the daily spiritual battle.

Imparted Righteousness

But the Bible also says, "Put on the full armor of God, so that you will be able to stand firm" (Ephesians 6:11 NASB). And, "Resist the devil and he will flee from you" (James 4:7). In other words, we don't passively rest in God's protection; we must also actively engage the Enemy in both offensive and defensive warfare, which means we need a second layer of protective righteousness. That is imparted righteousness: the active living out of a righteous lifestyle as a result of the working of God in our lives.

We are on dangerous ground here, however, because the one thing we do not want to say is that we can earn favor with God by being good. We can't. We don't want to say that we increase our chances of going to heaven by being good. We don't. We don't want to say that God likes some of us better than others because we are better people. He doesn't. But we must say that when we become a child of God, He wants us to live like He does.

"But as he who called you is holy, you also be holy in all your conduct, because it is written, 'Be holy, for I am holy'" (1 Peter 1:15–16). Or, as Paul wrote in Ephesians 4:1, "I . . . beseech you to walk worthy of the calling with which you were called." Loosely paraphrased, that means, "Start living like committed Christians."

HOW DO WE PUT ON THE BREASTPLATE OF DAILY RIGHTEOUS LIVING?

We don the breastplate of daily righteous living by being faithfully
obedient to all we understand Christ is asking of us.

When we become Christians, we begin to desire to do good things and avoid bad things—that's the Holy Spirit working within us. Often embryonic at first, this desire grows as we study the Bible and are challenged by the lives of others around us. The seeds of spiritual maturity must be watered and tended so that they take root and bear fruit in due season.

We keep short accounts with God. Everyone sins, and when we do we confess it and He is faithful and just, through our advocate Jesus Christ the righteous, to forgive our sin and cleanse us from all unrighteousness.

As the grace of God allows us, we live as righteous a life as we can. And that imparted righteousness protects us from the wiles of Satan.

We must count on our imputed righteousness and live out on a daily basis the righteousness that Christ imparts to us. To fool around with sin, to knowingly and willingly tolerate sin in our lives, breaches our defenses and makes us vulnerable in the spiritual battle.

HOW DOES SIN HURT US?

Sin hurts us by inflicting predictably painful consequences.

Many years ago, the Christian mandate for many believers consisted of a list of don'ts: don't go to movies, don't dance, don't drink, don't play cards, don't wear long hair, don't listen to rock 'n' roll music. Some of these prohibitions made good sense, while others were somewhat arbitrary.

WHY I NEED TO KNOW THIS

Today, there is a greatly diminished concern about righteousness. Christians tend to be more concerned about "not hurting" and about being personally fulfilled. They often follow non-scriptural means to achieve these two ends. However, God is concerned that we live righteous lives, and may bring whatever is necessary into our lives in order to lead us in that direction. We should be concerned about living righteously not only because that pleases God, but also because to fail to do so brings unnecessary and avoidable pain into our lives.

In the Christian circles in which I moved when I became a Christian, nothing was ever said about short tempers, but a lot was said about long hair. You couldn't see *The Sound of Music* in a movie theater, but you could watch anything you wanted on television. The Christian life was measured by the activities you didn't do, rather than by the Christlikeness of what you did do. If the sins were easily defined and visible, you couldn't do them. If they were not so easily defined or discernable, little was said.

In the last twenty years, that kind of legalism has been pretty much discarded except in some isolated circles. But in throwing out the bath water, we may have pitched the baby too. Now we want no one looking over our shoulders telling us what to do. But have we, in the name of Christian freedom, gone too far? Are we, in the name of Christian liberty, embracing many of the values of the world we are trying to redeem?

The Bible says it is a shame even to speak of the sins of immorality committed by the world (Ephesians 5:12). So is it legalism to exhort people not to watch those sins on television or in the movies?

The Bible says we are to think only about things that are true, honorable, right, pure, lovely, and of good repute (Philippians 4:8). So is it legalism to encourage people to guard themselves against the impure, the unlovely, and the dishonorable?

The Bible says we are to speak only that which is edifying to those who hear (Ephesians 4:29). So is it legalism to urge people to guard their tongues?

The Bible says the Lord hates dishonest business practices and a lying tongue (Proverbs 12:22; 16:11). So is it legalism to exhort people to be honest and ethical in the workplace?

No, it is not legalism to exhort ourselves and others to righteous behavior based on biblical principles. God has given us standards of righteous behavior to protect us, to glorify Him, and to be a witness to the world around us.

CONCLUSION

We are in a spiritual war, and Satan's two-pronged attack has strewn the battlefield around us with bleeding bodies.

First, Satan wages war on the battlefront of doctrinal purity. Then when he sees that we can hold our own there, he leaves some of his troops to keep us pinned down, outflanks us with the rest, and attacks from the rear. We now find ourselves losing the battle, not so much on the front of doctrinal purity as on the front of personal piety.

Today, we are in a unique position in church history: we have a generation of Christians who believe the historically accepted orthodoxy while adopting lifestyles that deny the very truth they allegedly embrace. They sincerely believe one thing, but live another. The divorce rate among Christians is the same as among non-Christians. Alcoholism and sexual abuse are nearly as prevalent within the church as without. The "health and wealth" gospel commands a strong following, materialism is at an all-time high, while personal discipline is at an all-time low. All of this and more has caused the church to lose its credibility as a significant force in American life. Many regard Christianity as an irrelevant belief because Christians don't exhibit it as a way of life.

If we don't want to be a war casualty, we must put on the breastplate of righteousness. We had better quit playing fast and loose with the Christian disciplines and the commands of Christ. We had better stop saying, "What can I get away with?" and start saying, "What would Jesus do?" We had better stop crying "legalism" and start proclaiming "righteousness." In spiritual warfare we need the protection of the breastplate of righteousness, not only out of respect for God and His commandments, but also for our own good. Everything God asks of us, He asks because He wants to give something good to us and keep some harm from us.

SPEED BUMP!

Slow down long enough to be sure you've gotten the main points of this chapter.

Q1. What does the breastplate of righteousness picture?

A1. The breastplate of righteousness pictures a *lifestyle* of trusting obedience to God.

Q2. What are the two dimensions of righteousness?

A2. Righteousness is both *imputed* and *imparted*.

Q3. How do we put on the breastplate of daily righteous living?

A3. We don the breastplate of daily righteous living by being faithfully *obedient* to all we understand Christ is asking of us.

Q4. How does sin hurt us?

A4. Sin hurts us by inflicting predictably painful *consequences*.

FILL IN THE BLANK

Q1 What does the breastplate of righteousness picture?

A1. The breastplate of righteousness pictures a _____ of trusting obedience to God.

Q2. What are the two dimensions of righteousness?

A2. Righteousness is both _____ and _____.

Q3. How do we put on the breastplate of daily righteous living?

A3. We don the breastplate of daily righteous living by being faithfully _____ to all we understand Christ is asking of us.

Q4. How does sin hurt us?

A4. Sin hurts us by inflicting predictably painful _____.

FOR FURTHER THOUGHT AND DISCUSSION

1. How have you seen God's commands protect your life? Have you experienced harm when you disobeyed His commands? Explain.

2. Do you see any areas in which, in the name of Christian freedom, you may have gone too far? Explain.

3. If Jesus were to visit you personally today, what do you think He would say about righteousness in your life?

WHAT IF I DON'T BELIEVE?

1. Living a righteous life can be very difficult and involves making some self-sacrificing decisions. If I don't believe that a righteous life is necessary to be pleasing to God as well as being self-fulfilling, I will not be willing to make the difficult decisions necessary.

2. Sin always has predictable negative consequences. If I am not willing to commit myself to a righteous lifestyle, I will bring unnecessary and avoidable pain into my life. The cost of righteousness may be high from time to time, but the cost of sin is always higher.

3. Righteousness is harder up front, but easier down the road. Sin is easier up front, but much harder down the road. Unless I understand that, I may choose to sin, thinking it is the easy way out. In the end, it is the hard way out.

4. If I do not commit myself to a life of righteousness, I am an easy target for spiritual deception. I become vulnerable to the wiles of the devil and throw open the door for his destructive work in my life.

FOR FURTHER STUDY

1. Scripture

Several Scripture passages speak of the importance of righteousness:

- Romans 12:1–2
- 1 Corinthians 9:24–27
- Ephesians 6:14
- Philippians 4:8–9
- 1 Peter 1:15–16

Read these passages and consider how they add to your understanding of the importance of righteousness.

2. Books

Several other books are very helpful in studying this subject. They are listed below in general order of difficulty.

30 Days to Understanding How to Live as a Christian, Max Anders

The Pursuit of Holiness, Jerry Bridges

The Practice of Godliness, Jerry Bridges

Growing in Christ, James I. Packer

Rediscovering Holiness, James I. Packer

5

This is a sane, wholesome, practical, working faith: That it is a man's business to do the will of God; second, that God himself takes on the care of that man; and third, that therefore that man ought never to be afraid of anything.
—**George MacDonald**

WHAT ARE THE SHOES OF THE GOSPEL OF PEACE?

Jumping backward off a cliff can teach you a lot about yourself. At least I've certainly found that it does. To be honest, the first time I didn't jump—it was more like a crawl. I was teaching at a college in Phoenix, Arizona, and one day several of my students approached me. "Mr. Anders," they said, "we are going up on Squaw Peak Mountain to do a little rappelling off some of the cliffs on Saturday. Would you like to go?"

It was hard for me to say no. For one thing, I didn't want to appear chicken. Besides, never having been rappelling before, I didn't understand how truly terrifying it would be. So I said yes.

When we got to the mountain the next Saturday, my companions chose "a small cliff." I'll never forget walking over to the edge and looking down for the first time—that small cliff was only about the height of a ten-story building! They tied a hundred-foot rope around a rock at the top, hooked themselves into harnesses, and started rappelling down the cliff.

There were about a half dozen of us, and because I wanted to be helpful, I let the others go first. Finally, I was the only one left. I muttered something about it taking longer than I expected and being a little short on time, but it didn't work. Before I knew what was happening, I was in a harness, and a rope the size of my first finger was threaded through and hanging off the cliff behind me.

By the time I got hooked up, most of the guys who had rappelled down had climbed back up to the top again, so there was a full house to witness my inauspicious descent.

"Just lean back against the rope, and walk backward off the cliff," they advised. Right!

I didn't trust the rope. Back in Indiana we used to swing on barn ropes that were as big around as my wrist. Those would hold a guy. This little thing might hold; it might not. And the aluminum safety pins (carabiners) that held me in my seat belt diaper and attached me to the rope—well, they didn't look strong enough to hold a Thanksgiving turkey. I didn't have faith in my equipment, and I was terrified.

But there I was. Halfway over the edge. Too proud to climb back up; too scared to lean back and walk off. So I began to sort of shinny down, holding the ropes so tightly that I didn't even need any equipment. With my legs wrapped around the rope, hunched over in a strange, modified fetal position, down over the edge I squirmed. It was not a pretty sight, but it was the best I could do.

Before I had gotten a third of the way down, my arms were trembling uncontrollably and almost useless. My kneecaps were scraped raw from rubbing against the face of the cliff; my hands and elbows were bruised and aching. I hung there like a ham in a smokehouse, lips and cheek pressed against the face of the cliff, wondering if I would live to see another sunrise.

With infinite patience, the leader of the group said, "Mr. Anders, let the rope hold you. Lean back into the rope until your feet are flat against the cliff like you are walking. Then just feed the rope through your hand and you will walk down the face of the cliff."

Finally, when I concluded that I would never get out of that alive anyway, I did what he said. I leaned back against the rope until my feet were flat against the face of the cliff. Then I let the rope out . . . and I walked effortlessly down the face of the cliff!

What an exhilarating experience. I couldn't wait to get back up to the top and try it again. This time I leaned back into the rope and walked over the edge of the cliff backward. I pushed myself away from the face of the cliff and free-fell for fifteen to twenty feet; then I bounced back to the cliff, pushed away again, and fell another fifteen to twenty feet. In probably no more than thirty seconds I was at the bottom, unhooking, and racing to the top to go down again.

What I learned that day was that you have to trust your rope. You have to believe that it will hold you. If you trust in your own strength to get you down, it will sap every molecule of power before you even get close to the ground. But if you let the rope do the work, you can make it.

When it comes to the spiritual life, we are like rappellers. The cliff is life. The rope is God. If we try to make it in our own strength, it will sap the life out of us. But if we lean back on the rope, believing that He will hold us, we let God do the work of God, and we make it down the cliff of life.

The apostle Paul tells us that there is an invisible army of evil beings that does the bidding of Satan and tries to thwart the will of God in the lives of Christians. Paul describes this as a spiritual battle, and he says there are six pieces of armor we need if we are to be victors. Thus far we have discussed the belt of truth and the breastplate of righteousness. Now we are going to look at the shoes of the gospel of peace. As in rappelling we gain peace by trusting our rope, so in life we gain peace by trusting in the promises of God.

WHAT DO THE SHOES OF THE GOSPEL OF PEACE PICTURE?

The shoes of the gospel of peace picture a trusting confidence in the promises of God, and the sense of peace that such trust brings.

. . . having shod your feet with the preparation of the gospel of peace (Ephesians 6:15).

The Roman soldier needed good footwear. A soldier who can't keep his footing is a vulnerable soldier. Josephus, in the sixth volume of his major work *The Jewish War*, describes the soldiers' footwear as "shoes thickly-studded with sharp nails." Thus, they could keep their footing in the worst conditions. The military successes of Alexander the Great and Julius Caesar were due largely to their armies' ability to undertake long marches at incredible speed over rough terrain. They could not have done this unless their feet were well shod. The same holds true in the spiritual battle. We must keep our footing, no matter how treacherous the ground.

When we investigate what the gospel of peace is, it helps to begin by saying what it is not. It is probably not the gospel message of salvation by grace through faith in Christ. The context here in Ephesians refers to things we do on a daily basis in spiritual battle. We do not become Christians anew every day; that happens once. Besides, little scriptural evidence suggests that sharing the gospel of salvation brings peace to the one who shares it.

> **Proper footwear is necessary for standing firm.**

What it does refer to, I believe, is the peace of God: the peace that is ours when we believe the promises of God and act accordingly. This is the peace suggested by Ephesians 2:14, where it describes Jesus Himself as being our peace. This is reinforced in John 14:27, where we read Jesus' own words: "Peace I leave with you, My peace I give to you; not as the world gives do I give to you. Let not your heart be troubled, neither let it be afraid."

This peace is central to fighting effectively in the spiritual war. So the truth here would be paraphrased: *the peace of God in your heart, which comes by resting in His promises, helps you stand firm in spiritual battle.*

When we believe what God says and trust Him, then we have the personal, inner peace that enables us to keep our footing in the daily spiritual battle. If we do not believe the promises of God, we will become agitated, weakened, and confused; when that happens, we are likely to lose our footing, lose ground, and eventually be defeated in the war against Satan.

HOW DO GOD'S PROMISES GIVE US PEACE?

God's promises give us peace by answering our greatest fears.

Let's look at three of God's most important promises as examples, and see how they give us the inner peace we need to stand firm.

1. God's Promise to Give Us Eternal Life

For God so loved the world that He gave His only begotten Son, that whoever believes in Him should not perish but have eternal life (John 3:16).

Everyone, at one time or another, thinks about death, and everyone, at one time or another, is afraid to die.

Pogo, a philosophizing possum in the Sunday cartoons, who lived in the Okefenokee Swamp, once said: "I hate death. In fact, I could live forever without it." Film director Woody Allen said: "It's not that I'm afraid to die. I just don't want to be there when it happens." And the little child says: "Dear God, what is it like when you die? Nobody will tell me. I just want to *know*. I don't want to *do* it."

Actually, most of the time the very young and the very old tend to think about dying. Everyone in between thinks about death only when they are very sick or when someone else dies or is in a bad accident. For most people, death is a swirling, yawning black hole at the end of the conveyor belt of life. People ride along on the conveyor belt, and when they get to the end, the belt drops them off into this black hole. Death is the great unknown.

IN THIS CHAPTER WE LEARN THAT . . .

1. The shoes of the gospel of peace picture a trusting confidence in the promises of God and the sense of peace that such trust brings.

2. God's promises give us peace by answering our greatest fears.

3. God's promises lighten our load by helping us lay down burdens that God never intended us to carry.

What happens then? This is, of course, the greatest question everyone asks. It is the question around which much of our literature and art is created and framed.

Is there a God? Is there life after death? Is there a heaven? Is there a hell? If there might be, where am I going to go? Is it safe to die? Is there the possibility of eternal torment? How can I escape it? How can I know for sure?

Someone has described death this way:

> Like a hen before a cobra, we find ourselves incapable of doing anything at all in the presence of the very thing that seems to call for the most drastic and decisive action. The disquieting thought, that stares at us like a face with a freezing grin, is that there is, in fact, nothing we can do. Say what we will, dance how we will, we will soon enough be a heap of ruined feathers and bones.

Undertaker or comedian, lawyer or pipe fitter, admiral or homemaker, mechanic or movie star, cowboy or congressman—get them in a quiet moment when they will talk honestly and openly with you, and the one thing nearly everyone fears most is death. The great enemy. The great unknown.

In the face of this reality, the great promise from Jesus is life. "*I am the resurrection and the life,*" He said. "*He who believes in Me, though he may die, he shall live. And whoever lives and believes in Me shall never die*" (John 11:25–26). If we believe in Jesus, it is safe to die. We don't have to fear the great unknown any longer. We can rest in His promise and have peace in the face of life's greatest enemy, death.

2. God's Promise to Guide Us in Daily Life

Trust in the LORD with all your heart, / And lean not on your own understanding; / In all your ways acknowledge Him, / And He shall direct your paths (Proverbs 3:5–6).

We don't have to know which way to go through life. All we have to do is keep our hand in the hand of the One who does. We don't have to stumble around, or stub our toe in the darkness, or walk off a cliff in blindness. The truth of the Scripture will give us light and sight and keep us from straying off the safe path.

There is an old saying: "In order to be free to sail the seven seas, we must make ourselves a slave to the compass." When we become slaves to Christ, we free ourselves to sail the seven seas of life. We don't have to be anchored to ignorance or unseemly desires or lies. There is no bondage in commitment to Christ, only freedom.

When we determine to follow all that we understand of God in the Scripture, we have peace—peace in knowing that we are doing the right thing with our life, peace in recognizing that God is pleased with us, peace in realizing that we are free from slavery to things that hurt us. God's will is good.

3. God's Promise to Give Us Peace in the Midst of Pain

And we know that all things work together for good to those who love God, to those who are the called according to His purpose (Romans 8:28).

Sooner or later, life will haul off and sock every one of us right in the stomach. And while we are standing there with pain stabbing our whole body, knees buckling, mouth agape, struggling for air, we all ask ourselves, "Why? . . . Why did *this* happen to me? Why did this happen to *me*? What sense does it make? What good can ever come out of this?"

Many things cause us pain, but we bring much of it on ourselves. Why? Because we do things the Bible warns us against. Thus we reap what we have sown.

Maybe in the past, a foolish act of yours resulted in more pain than you ever thought possible as you suffered consequences of your sin. Yet God can turn that into good by making you stronger, more insightful, more sensitive, and wiser. He can turn your heartbreak to good by using you in the lives of others as you share the wisdom you have learned and help them not to make the same mistake. God can transform your life into a glorious tribute to His grace no matter what you have done. He can bring good out of any pain.

WHY I NEED TO KNOW THIS

Peace is one of the great voids in the lives of many people. From the great social and political threats of terrorism, war, AIDS, and declining American culture, to the personal fears of death, finances, health, loneliness, purpose, and meaning, something in almost everyone's life threatens to rob that person of peace. The world has no way to give us peace. But Jesus promises to give us the peace we long for, if we but take Him at His word.

Sometimes pain results from God's spanking us. This kind of pain hurts just as much as other pain, but God is able to bring good out of it too. Hebrews 12:7, 11 says: "God deals with you as with sons; for what son is there whom a father does not chasten? . . . Now no chastening seems to be joyful for the present, but painful; nevertheless, afterward it yields the peaceable fruit of righteousness to those who have been trained by it."

Perhaps you started drinking, and before you knew it you were addicted. As a Christian, you knew it was wrong. You knew you were in trouble, but you were too proud to ask for help or to repent. In trying to fight it yourself, you lost. Soon you stopped trying to walk with God because you were convinced He was sick of you. You lost your friends, your job, even your family. You hit bottom.

Then, there on the bottom, you "found" God again. (Actually, He was there all the time, waiting.) You repented. You followed His leading and got the help you needed.

Now, years have gone by and you are still sober. God disciplined you. It hurt. But through it, God brought righteousness, strength, stability, and peace back into your life. And it is good.

Then, of course, there is the pain that no one can explain. The heartache for a wayward child, the agony of disease, the burden of a physical disability. Yet those who have passed through these can testify that often when the pain is greatest, Jesus is the closest. They will tell you that when they reflect on the work God did in their lives as a result, the suffering was worth it.

Sometimes a person doesn't gain this perspective and gratitude until afterward. At other times, fellowship with God is closest and sweetest in the very midst of the turmoil. But always, God can give peace for pain.

HOW DO GOD'S PROMISES LIGHTEN OUR LOAD?

God's promises lighten our load by helping us lay down
burdens that God never intended us to carry.

Often when life gets so heavy that it threatens to crush us, it is because we are trying to carry a burden Jesus never intended us to carry. The burden of trying to control all the people and possessions and circumstances to make life go the way we want it is too heavy for us. We cannot gain that much control. If we trust Him to guide us, we can have peace in the midst of life's uncertainties.

The burden of trying to cope with pain is often greater than we can handle by ourselves. If we trust Jesus to carry the load and give us the grace to face what comes, moment by moment, we can have peace in the midst of pain and beauty for ashes later.

Many of us must be brought to the end of our own spiritual and emotional resources and strength before we will lean back into Jesus, believe His promises, and rest in them. When we do, He gives us the peace that puts our feet on solid ground and enables us to stand firm in the spiritual battle.

When we put on the shoes of the gospel of peace, we are saying, "I believe the promises of God and count on them to be true for me. And when I do, I can have His peace in my life."

CONCLUSION

Bible students differ regarding what Paul meant when he said "having shod your feet with the preparation of the gospel of peace." This confusion arises primarily out of a passage in Romans 10:15 where Paul quoted Isaiah 52:7:

> How beautiful upon the mountains
> Are the feet of him who brings good news,
> Who proclaims peace,
> Who brings glad tidings of good things,
> Who proclaims salvation,
> Who says to Zion,
> "Your God reigns!"

Because of the similarity of this passage to "having shod your feet with the preparation of the gospel of peace," some have taken the Ephesians passage to mean that we should be "ever ready to share our faith with others" as part of our spiritual armor. John R. W. Stott comments that "such tip-toe readiness has a very stabilizing influence on our own lives, as well as [leading to our] introducing others to the liberating gospel" (*God's New Society*, 280).

Others, however, are less persuaded. Among these is John MacArthur:

> Because Paul quoted Isaiah 52:7 in the context of preaching the gospel (Romans 10:15), many commentators also interpret Ephesians 6:15 as a reference to preaching. But in the Ephesians text Paul is not talking about preaching or teaching but about fighting spiritual battles. His subject is not evangelizing the lost but fighting the devil. In this passage the gospel of peace refers to the good news that believers are at peace with God. (*Ephesians*, 355)

Both positions are responsible positions, and one would not go wrong holding to either one. Both positions (that we should embrace all the promises of God, and that we should be "tip-toe ready" to share the gospel with the unsaved) are true and are reinforced by other passages of Scripture. Regardless of which position you believe better fits Ephesians 6:15, as long as you also accept the scriptural truth of the other position, that piece of your armor will be firmly in place.

SPEED BUMP!

Slow down long enough to be sure you've gotten the main points of this chanter.

Q1. What do the shoes of the gospel of peace picture?

A1. The shoes of the gospel of peace picture a trusting confidence in the *promises* of God, and the sense of peace that such trust brings.

Q2. How do God's promises give us peace?

A2. God's promises give us peace by answering our greatest *fears*.

Q3. How do God's promises lighten our load?

A3. God's promises lighten our load by helping us lay down *burdens* that God never intended us to carry.

FILL IN THE BLANK

Q1. What do the shoes of the gospel of peace picture?

A1. The shoes of the gospel of peace picture a trusting confidence in the _____ of God, and the sense of peace that such trust brings.

Q2. How do God's promises give us peace?

A2. God's promises give us peace by answering our greatest _____.

Q3. How do God's promises lighten our load?

A3. God's promises lighten our load by helping us lay down _____ that God never intended us to carry.

FOR FURTHER THOUGHT AND DISCUSSION

1. What one thing do you fear most about totally trusting Christ? What would you need to do to totally trust Him in that area?

2. Do you think it is "safer" to trust Christ and obey Him or to distrust Him and disobey Him and try to control your own circumstances? This is especially difficult to answer when you think of something that Jesus might be asking of you that you don't want to do.

3. Which of the three promises in this chapter is hardest for you to rest in? Which is easiest? Explain why.

WHAT IF I DON'T BELIEVE?

1. If I don't believe and rest in the promises of God, my life is liable to be a constant stream of anxiety and distress.

2. If I don't accept the necessity of trusting God's character, I will be constantly tempted to question either the goodness of God, or His love for me.

3. If I am buffeted by a lack of peace and crushed by the constant weight of burdens God never intended me to carry, I become a target for Satan's deception.

FOR FURTHER STUDY

1. Scripture

Several Scripture passages speak of the peace that comes from trusting in the promises of God:

- Matthew 11:28–30
- John 14:27
- Ephesians 6:15
- Philippians 4:7
- 2 Thessalonians 3:16

Read these passages and consider how they add to your understanding of the importance of trusting in the promises of God.

2. Books

Several other books are very helpful in studying this subject. They are listed below in general order of difficulty.

30 Days to Understanding How to Live as a Christian, Max Anders

Joy That Lasts, Gary Smalley

6

WHAT IS THE SHIELD OF FAITH?

He that will not command his thoughts will soon lose command of his actions.
—**Woodrow Wilson**

In *Beyond Survival*, pilot Gerald Coffee tells of his shock in finding himself a prisoner of war in North Vietnam. February 3, 1966, dawned a dazzling bright day. Bombardier-navigator Bob Hanson and pilot Gerald Coffee made their way across the flight deck of the USS *Kitty Hawk* and manned their powerful jet aircraft for takeoff. Their thirty-ton reconnaissance jet roared to life and surged to 170 miles per hour in less than three seconds. Coffee eased the nose up into a climbing turn over the watery mirror below, the deep blue Gulf of Tonkin.

Coffee and Hanson were headed over North Vietnam for the second time, and their nerves were electrified. Everything was going like clockwork. Coffee caught the target bridge in the brackets of his viewfinder and snapped the recon photos he needed. All the while, he zig-zagged through the sky to keep enemy gunners below from getting a bead on him.

Just as it all seemed over, they were hit. Without warning, the great manned missile they were riding became sluggish and unresponsive. Like a living thing beginning to die, the plane rolled left and the nose dropped. It was headed, like a bomb, for the shimmering blue grave below.

"Eject, Bob! Eject! Eject!" Coffee screamed.

As I came awake, I sensed my surroundings more than I saw them. I was in a stable. A water buffalo stood nearby with the chickens scratching at its feet. I was struck with the dreamlike scene—the serenity of the animals, the low bubbling of an opium pipe, the mixture of smells, and finally the incongruity of my own presence. Here I was, 31 years old, a prisoner of war among people we had been bombing and strafing. God, I am going to need you a lot. Please stay with me. (26)

Similar stories were repeated frequently during the Southeast Asian conflict, and observers over the years have noted an interesting pattern. Of the many men who survived the horrors of captivity in Vietnam, those who survived well had at least two things in common: they had the ability to develop an inner world in which they lived, and throughout their ordeal they held on to the truth with bulldog tenacity.

IN THIS CHAPTER WE LEARN THAT . . .

1. The shield of faith pictures a life of protection based on our faith in God's character, Word, and deeds.

2. Faith is believing what God has said and committing ourselves to His word.

3. The Bible does not tell us specifically what Satan's flaming arrows are, though they can be anything that causes us to doubt or disobey the truth.

4. We use the shield of faith when we commit ourselves to live according to the truth of God's word instead of Satan's lies.

One POW was a piano player. He played concert after concert in his own mind to help pass the time. Another was an architect. He designed imaginary houses, buildings, and entire cities in his mind during his long incarceration. Another man was an avid golfer. He played golf day in and day out on the golf courses in his memory. Curiously enough, after he got back to the United States and had recovered his health, he discovered that he was a better golfer than he was before he went to Vietnam! These POWs constructed mental games and inner worlds to help them cope with both the horrors and the boredom of captivity.

Standard operating procedure for the Vietnamese was to try to break their prisoners mentally. To do this, hour after hour they would pump propaganda into the prisoners' cells via radio, loud speakers, and interrogators. Telling them that the United States government was a government of monsters . . . that the U.S. military had already forgotten them . . . that they were listed as killed in action and that no attempt whatsoever was being made to free them . . . that their families were no longer concerned about them . . . that their families didn't want to wait for them to get out of prison . . . that their wives had already divorced them and remarried.

The POWs able to resist this type of brainwashing were those who caught these lies in midair, slammed them to the ground, and kicked them out of their mind. They would remind themselves of the truth, force themselves to cling to it, and answer every lie with a corresponding truth.

No, they haven't forgotten me! . . . No, they haven't given me up as dead . . . They will come back and get me . . . No, that isn't true. It's a propaganda ploy . . . My wife hasn't remarried anyone else. She still loves me. She's going to wait for me till I get out.

By focusing on their inner world and clinging tenaciously to truth, these men were able not only to survive a brutal captivity but also, after their release, to put the war behind them, pick up their lives, and again become productive and happy members of society. Their battle was not just physical; it was a battle of the mind and spirit.

Each believer faces exactly the same thing in spiritual warfare. We do not live solely in the physical realm. We are surrounded by the forces of darkness, poised to do whatever they can to thwart the will of God in our lives. Continuing in Paul's imagery of the Roman soldier, we look at the next piece of the armor of God, the shield of faith.

WHAT DOES THE SHIELD OF FAITH PICTURE?

*The shield of faith pictures a life of protection based on our
faith in God's character, Word, and deeds.*

. . . taking up the shield of faith with which you will be able to extinguish all the flaming arrows of the evil one (Ephesians 6:16 NASB).

Roman soldiers sometimes used a small, round shield, but the Greek word translated here describes a shield large enough for several soldiers to crouch behind to protect themselves from volleys of arrows coming from enemy archery divisions. The surface of these large shields was either metal or leather-covered wood that could also repel or withstand flaming arrows. These were arrows that had been soaked in or wrapped with flammable material and were then set on fire and launched by the enemy—they were doubly lethal.

In spiritual warfare the enemy of our soul launches his deadly missiles at us, and it is faith that protects us. Faith is our shield.

WHAT IS FAITH?

Faith is believing what God has said and committing ourselves to His Word.

The world's definition of faith is *believing in spite of the fact that there is nothing to believe.* But that is not the biblical description of faith.

Faith is believing what God has said. For example, God has said He will never leave us or forsake us. He has said that He will take care of all our needs. So anytime we are believing something God has said, we are exercising faith.

But faith goes beyond mere belief. In fact, faith is not faith until it exercises commitment.

Do you believe in Jesus? That is intellectual belief, and it is not enough. That is believing *about* Jesus. You must believe *in* Jesus. Only when you have committed your life to Him and to the truth He taught do you believe *in* Him. That is faith.

The shield of faith means that we are protected by the truth of Scripture and the power of God when we believe what God says and commit ourselves to it.

WHAT ARE THE FLAMING ARROWS?

The Bible does not tell us specifically what Satan's flaming arrows are, though they can be anything that causes us to doubt or disobey the truth.

Most commentators say the flaming arrows are discouragement, doubt, fear, hate, desire, lust, and possibly procrastination and carelessness. With the shield of faith we can extinguish these burning arrows of the evil one. So if we find ourselves in the middle of something that we cannot extinguish, it is probably not a flaming arrow.

For example, many Christians died during the persecution of the Jews in Nazi Germany. That persecution was described as a flaming arrow. Although great faith was exercised in the midst of that persecution, the persecution was not extinguished. It went on for years. Therefore, I would suggest that this persecution was not in itself a flaming arrow.

However, in the midst of that persecution, Satan could have launched flaming arrows of doubt and discouragement and bitter thoughts against God. Those are the kinds of fiery darts that Satan would delight in hurling at believers in the midst of such extreme suffering. And those are the kinds of evil-inspired flaming arrows that can be extinguished and vanquished by faith: doubt, discouragement, bitterness, and hate.

HOW DO WE USE THE SHIELD OF FAITH?

We use the shield of faith when we commit ourselves to live according to the truth of God's Word instead of Satan's lies.

Flaming arrows are thoughts and feelings that Satan projects into our minds to get us to doubt what God has said. Often Satan or his emissaries hurl their fiery darts in such a way that when they enter your mind, you end up saying, "I think this . . ." or, "I feel that . . ."

Use faith as a shield, then, calling the lie a lie, and telling yourself the truth! Let's look at several examples.

Discouragement

You have been married for five years and things are not going just the way you would like. Satan comes along and prompts you to say, "I'm discouraged. My marriage is not as rewarding as I thought it was going to be. Maybe I married the wrong person. Maybe God really wanted me to marry someone else. I would be better off if I were married to someone else."

The shield of faith says, "No. That is a lie. I prayed for God's guidance before we got married. Our parents and pastor gave us their blessing. I was not living in any known sin. So I must accept that it was God's will for me to marry my spouse. I vowed to remain faithful, and God expects me to keep that vow. He will strengthen me to do His will. If I am honest, I will have to say that many of the problems in our marriage are my own fault, and I must uphold my end of the relationship better. If I trust and obey God, He will use this time of testing to build my spiritual maturity." That's the shield of faith. It catches Satan's lies in midair, kicks them out, and tells the truth.

Temptation

You are traveling on business for your company, and you have an expense account of $150 a day for food and lodging. You got a good deal on a hotel room, and you ate one meal on the plane, so for today you have spent only $100. When you asked for a receipt from the taxi driver, he tore off a blank receipt form and told you to fill in the amount yourself. When you asked for a receipt after your meal, the waitress simply tore off the bottom of the check and gave it to you blank. Now you are sitting in your room at the end of the day, tallying up your records and considering the $50 you could put in your pocket by padding your expense account.

> ### WHY I NEED TO KNOW THIS
>
> In order to exercise biblical faith, I need to know what it is and what it is not. To be able to exercise biblical faith, I need to trust in the character of God. I can never trust fully someone whose character I doubt. Satan and his demons will try their hardest to get me to doubt God's character and give up on faith. To be forewarned is to be forearmed. I need to know this so that Satan will not get the upper hand in my life.

Satan has you thinking, *Go ahead, for heaven's sake. It's only $50. It's not like I'm going to break the company. Besides, everyone does it—even the president of the company. So why in the world wouldn't it be okay for me to do it? Nobody is going to know, and $50 isn't going to hurt anything in a $100 million operation.*

The shield of faith says: "No! The Bible says I should not steal. God hates dishonesty and falsehood. The Bible says the person who conceals his or her sin will not prosper. The Bible says God will supply all my needs in Christ Jesus. I will not steal this money."

That's the shield of faith in operation. It catches Satan's lies in midair, kicks them out, and tells the truth.

Immorality

You have been traveling all day. You have checked into your hotel, had a bite to eat in the coffee shop, and are now relaxing in your room for a couple of hours before hitting the sack. You turn on the TV and start flipping through the channels. NBC, CBS, ABC, Playboy. What's this? The Playboy channel? There's no box on top of the TV, which means you don't have to pay for it. It's just there, like ABC and all the rest.

Satan starts you musing, *There it is—two hours of free lust. Go ahead. The door is locked. The curtains are pulled. No one will ever know. After all, I'm just a healthy, red-blooded American man. Everybody from congressmen to businessmen to some preachers watch this kind of stuff. I've always been curious—I'll just check this stuff out and see what it's like. Besides, no one will ever know. And a couple hours can't hurt. It's just like watching a movie.*

The shield of faith replies, "It's a sin against God. It's a sin against my wife. It will make me more susceptible next time, and it can become an addiction. It will inhibit my relationship with my wife. The Bible says, 'Be holy for I am holy.' The Bible says I must love my wife as Christ loved the church. The Bible says, 'Whatever a man sows, that shall he also reap.' I would be sowing infidelity, dishonesty, and lust. What possible good can come from that? Besides, it will not satisfy. It will only create a desire for more, and I cannot satisfy that desire without getting in deeper and deeper until in the end I will be addicted and destroyed."

That's the shield of faith. It catches Satan's lies in midair, kicks them out, and tells the truth.

Doubt

Life is a mess. It's so unfair. After a tempestuous courtship and a brief marriage, your husband divorced you. Now he is out running around with as many women as he can. You are working two low-paying jobs just to make ends meet. At the day's end, you are so tired there is no chance of meaningful interaction. You are getting old before your time. You'd like to remarry, but none of the men you are interested in is interested in you.

Satan has you wallowing in self-pity. *God doesn't love me. There's something wrong with me. If God really loved me, He wouldn't treat me this way. What have I done to deserve this? Life just isn't fair. Christianity doesn't work. It's a religion for suckers, and I've been suckered long enough. My ex is out there, carefree, living the good life. Why shouldn't I go out and get myself a piece of the action for a change? If I don't look out for myself, no one else will.*

The shield of faith says, "No! That's a lie. It is true that my life hasn't been a bed of roses, but much of my trouble I have caused myself. I knew I shouldn't have married Jim; I knew he wasn't a committed Christian. Besides, I wasn't the perfect wife. And since the divorce I haven't really gotten involved in a church where I could have some spiritual accountability and relationships with godly people. I have not been careful to do what the Bible says. God does not hate me. He loves me, and He has sent people to help me—like my parents—but I didn't listen to them. I am paying the consequences for my bad choices. But I can begin to walk a different path. I can begin by committing my life totally to Christ. When I do, God will bring His truth and His people and His blessing into my life and help me get it turned around."

CONCLUSION

That's the shield of faith. It catches Satan's lies in midair, kicks them out, and tells the truth. Anything we are tempted to do short of total commitment to Christ is a lie. It is Satan's spiritual brainwashing. He wants to deceive us in order to destroy us. What he offers never satisfies nor gives us the peace we long for; it only makes us want the next lower level he has to offer. Then, when that doesn't satisfy—which it never does—it leads us deeper still. And so it goes, on and on, until he has us addicted and destroyed.

When faced with Satan's lies, we must say, "No. That is a lie and I am not going to believe it. I am tired of your yanking me around by your lies and promises of better things if I take shortcuts. I am going to do what I know is right, I'm going to tell myself the truth, and for now and for all in my life, I am going to do what is right."

When you do that, you come under the umbrella of God's protection and guidance. And though it may take some time to clear up all the messes, God will straighten out your life and make something beautiful out of it.

Don't settle for anything less than believing God and doing what He says. You're worth far too much to waste yourself on anything other than Him.

When we take up the shield of faith, we are saying, "Whenever I feel like doubting or sinning or quitting, I will reject those thoughts and feelings because I deeply believe in God's truth."

SPEED BUMP!

Slow down long enough to be sure you've gotten the main points of this chapter.

Q1. What does the shield of faith picture?

A1. The shield of faith pictures a life of protection based on our *faith* in God's character, word, and deeds.

Q2. What is faith?

A2. Faith is *believing* what God has said and *committing* ourselves to His Word.

Q3. What are the flaming arrows?

A3. The Bible does not tell us specifically what Satan's flaming arrows are, though they can be anything that causes us to *doubt* or disobey the truth.

Q4. How do we use the shield of faith?

A4. We use the shield of faith when we *commit* ourselves to live according to the truth of God's Word instead of Satan's lies.

FILL IN THE BLANK

Q1. What does the shield of faith picture?

A1. The shield of faith pictures a life of protection based on our _____ in God's character, word, and deeds.

Q2. What is faith?

A2. Faith is _____ what God has said and _____ ourselves to His word.

Q3. What are the flaming arrows?

A3. The Bible does not tell us specifically what Satan's flaming arrows are, though they can be anything that causes us to _____ or disobey the truth.

Q4. How do we use the shield of faith?

A4. We use the shield of faith when we _____ ourselves to live according to the truth of God's Word instead of Satan's lies.

FOR FURTHER THOUGHT AND DISCUSSION

1. Can you think of any areas in your life where you have been believing Satan's lies?

2. What is the truth that contradicts those lies?

3. Do you think you know the Bible well enough to use Scripture to counter Satan's lies? What is the most important thing you could do to improve your command of Scripture?

WHAT IF I DON'T BELIEVE?

1. If I don't realize that the entire Christian faith and walk is based on faith—believing God and acting accordingly—then my entire Christian walk will be skewed.

2. I will be continually frustrated and confused over God's refusal to bless things I cherish.

3. I will be powerless to withstand the doubts, temptations, and discouragements that are a given in the Christian life.

4. The worst-case scenario is that I would abandon the Christian faith altogether.

FOR FURTHER STUDY

1. Scripture

Several Scripture passages speak of the importance of faith:

- Matthew 17:20
- Romans 5:1
- Romans 10:17
- Ephesians 6:14
- Hebrews 11:1
- Hebrews 11:6
- James 1:3

Read these passages and consider how they add to your understanding of faith.

2. Books

Several other books are very helpful in studying this subject. They are listed below in general order of difficulty.

30 Days to Understanding How to Live as a Christian, Max Anders
How to Meet the Enemy, John MacArthur
Spiritual Warfare, Ray Stedman

7

WHAT IS THE HELMET OF SALVATION?

Aim at heaven, and you will get earth thrown in. Aim at earth, and you get neither.
—C. S. Lewis

Charles Dickens's *A Christmas Carol* is, aside from the Christmas story in the Gospels, probably the most beloved of all Christmas stories. Whether being read aloud by the glow of Christmas lights or enjoyed in one of its many film versions, the story of stingy Scrooge, frail Tiny Tim, sturdy Bob Cratchit, and the three Christmas ghosts warms our hearts and renews our spirits.

Scrooge, led by the Ghosts of Christmas Past, Present, and Future, was able to see what he had been, what he had become, and what the future held for him unless he changed his ways. He was shown the future before it happened, and as a result, was able to alter the future in a positive way by changing his present behavior. In a sense, the story expresses a nice metaphor for the Holy Spirit who has been sent to guide us into all truth—and the source of that truth, the Word of God.

The Bible reveals the future to us and makes clear that who we are and what we do now has eternal consequences. We must fix a picture of eternity in our minds and live today in light of who we have become and who we will be when we get to heaven. We must live in this world according to the value system of the next.

Alexander Solzhenitsyn said, "The only way to survive in prison is to abandon all expectations for this world and live for the next." The only way to have consistent joy in this life is to place our values, our hopes, our expectations, and our affections in the next world, not this one.

WHAT DOES THE HELMET OF SALVATION PICTURE?

*The helmet of salvation pictures a lifestyle of hope that comes
from focusing on our ultimate salvation.*

And take the helmet of salvation . . . (Ephesians 6:17a).

The head is a particularly vulnerable spot on the human body. A blow to the arm or leg may be painful but a blow to the head brings stars exploding and birds singing. A sharp blow to the arm or leg might break a bone; a sharp blow to the head can kill. That is why football players and bicycle riders wear helmets, and construction workers don hard hats.

For obvious reasons, Roman soldiers wore helmets. A blow from a sword, spear, or club could cause injury or death, so the soldier preparing for battle protected his head with a helmet. And in developing his metaphor of spiritual armor, Paul indicates that the helmet is one of the most important pieces, for it is the helmet of salvation.

Salvation has three different dimensions: past, present, and future.

Past: "For by grace you *have been saved* through faith, and that not of yourselves; it is the gift of God, not of works, lest anyone should boast" (Ephesians 2:8–9, emphasis mine).

This implies that at some point in the past we were forgiven and cleansed of our sins, spiritually reborn, and made eligible for heaven. We were justified—declared righteous—by God.

IN THIS CHAPTER WE LEARN THAT . . .

1. The helmet of salvation pictures a lifestyle of hope that comes from focusing on our ultimate salvation.

2. We cultivate an eternal perspective by viewing all temporal things in light of eternity.

3. I transfer my hope from this world to the next by using the disappointments of this world as a catalyst to consciously embrace God's answer to those disappointments.

Past salvation delivered us from the *penalty* of sin.

Present: "For the message of the cross is foolishness to those who are perishing, but to us who *are being saved* it is the power of God" (1 Corinthians 1:18, emphasis added).

This conveys the idea that we are being freed more and more from the power of sin in our everyday lives. Jesus said, "You shall know the truth, and the truth shall make you free" (John 8:32). As we come to know more and more truth, we are set more and more free from the negative effects of sin. As we live in faithful obedience to God, He liberates us from the power and bondage of sin.

When God requires us to be faithful in marriage to only one person and not to be sexually promiscuous, He is freeing us from deadly diseases. When He asks us not to get drunk, He is turning us loose from the devastation of alcohol abuse. When He asks us to control our anger, He is delivering us from the effects of physical and emotional abuse.

While many think only of the high cost of being a disciple, they forget about the high cost of *not* being a disciple.

Present salvation delivers us from the *power* of sin.

Future: "Christ also, having been offered once to bear the sins of many, will appear a second time for salvation without reference to sin, to those who eagerly await Him" (Hebrews 9:28 NASB).

When Christ comes again, He will deliver us to our final salvation, and we will go to heaven. The present heaven and earth will be destroyed in a cosmic flash, and a new heaven and earth will be created. All sin will be destroyed, and we will live forever in the presence of God, unaffected and untouched by sin, never again knowing anything of it.

When Paul mentions the helmet of salvation as being our next piece of spiritual armor, he is not talking about our past salvation in which we experienced conversion in Christ. He's not looking back. Rather, he's looking forward to our future salvation and to the hope it brings.

This forward look is clear in 1 Thessalonians 5:8: "But let us who are of the day be sober, putting on the breastplate of faith and love, and *as a helmet the hope of salvation*" (emphasis mine). This Thessalonian "spiritual armor" section is written to people who are already saved. If someone has already taken up the belt of truth and the breastplate of righteousness, he is saved, even before he dons his helmet. It would be redundant to add a helmet to the belt of truth and breastplate of righteousness if he were referring to past salvation from the penalty of sin. Instead, Paul is looking forward to believers' ultimate salvation from the presence of sin and the hope that it gives for the trials of today.

Hope is absolutely essential to keep going in any endeavor. It is when people lose all hope that they commit suicide. To ask someone to live without hope is like asking someone to run a race that doesn't have a finish line. Knowing that there is a finish line and where it is gives us the strength to keep running. When we can look forward to our ultimate redemption and to the fulfillment of our heart's greatest longing, then we can have hope in this life that strengthens us to endure the difficulties.

Understood in that way, it makes perfect sense for Paul to encourage us to take up this piece of armor as part of our ongoing spiritual battle. The battle will seem like no more than a second compared to eternity. Or as Mother Teresa put it, when we get to heaven, all our worst experiences on earth will seem like no more than a bad night in a cheap hotel.

Many Scripture verses confirm this. For example, we have the wonderful confidence of knowing that we cannot lose the fight we're in. In Romans 8:30, Paul says that whom God "predestined, these He also called; whom He called, these He also justified; these He also glorified." These are the wonderful secure links in our chain of salvation. There is not one break from predestination to glorification.

This salvation gives us what Peter calls a "living hope."

> Blessed be the God and Father of our Lord Jesus Christ, who according to His abundant mercy has begotten us again to a living hope through the resurrection of Jesus Christ from the dead, to an inheritance incorruptible and undefiled and that does not fade away, reserved in heaven for you, who are kept by the power of God through faith for salvation ready to be revealed in the last time. (1 Peter 1:3–5)

When we have this living hope, Peter goes on to write that

> In this you greatly rejoice, though now for a little while, if need be, you have been grieved by various trials, that the genuineness of your faith, being much more precious than gold that perishes, though it is tested by fire, may be found to praise, honor, and glory at the revelation of Jesus Christ, whom having not seen you love. Though now you do not see Him, yet believing, you rejoice with joy inexpressible and full of glory, receiving the end of your faith—the salvation of your souls. (vv. 1:6–9)

As we see, biblical hope is more than wishful thinking, even earnest wishful thinking. Often when people hope for something, they express it this way: "I sure hope we win the game" (or get my promotion or get a clean bill of health from the doctor). Nothing is wrong with such hope, but it is not what the New Testament is talking about. Instead, "hope" in the New Testament means the certainty God deposits in our hearts that He will fulfill all His great and precious promises in His time and way. It is easy to see how this kind of hope—this kind of forward-leaning confidence—gives us steadfastness, strength, courage, and endurance in the face of life's great trials.

Throughout Scripture we see the promise and description of the future blessings of our salvation as giving us hope and even joy and exaltation. In Romans 5:2, Paul wrote, "We . . . rejoice in hope of the glory of God." We confidently look forward one day to shedding our body in which the power of sin still resides (Romans 7) and to finally becoming fully glorified persons free to worship God without any limitations of sin. Our greatest hopes, our deepest joys, our highest longings will be realized. And our by-faith certainty of their realization is "hope."

But Paul didn't end there in Romans 5:2, but went on in verses 3 and 4 to write, "And not only that, but we also glory in tribulations, knowing that tribulation produces perseverance; and perseverance, character; and character, hope. Now hope does not disappoint, because the love of God has been poured out in our hearts by the Holy Spirit who was given to us."

A Christian can rejoice not only because he or she looks forward with confident anticipation to the future glory God has promised, but also while in the reality of present trials. Why? Because these trials produce character that has the capacity to rejoice in the future. These trials produce a character full of hope—confidence that God will finally give us everything He has promised.

In her book *A Step Further*, Joni Eareckson Tada wrote:

> No, Satan doesn't sneak out and cause pneumonia and cancer while God happens to be looking the other way listening to the prayers of his saints. He can only do what our all-powerful and all-knowing God allows him to do. And we have God's promise that nothing will be allowed which is not for our good or which is too hard for us to bear (Romans 8:28; 1 Corinthians 10:13). . . .
>
> Praise God that when Satan causes us illness—or any calamity, we can answer him with the words Joseph answered his brothers who sold him into slavery, "As for you, you meant evil against me, but God meant it for good" (Genesis 50:20).
>
> I sometimes shudder to think where I would be today if I had not broken my neck. I couldn't see at first why God would possibly allow it, but I sure do now. He has gotten so much more glory through my paralysis than through my health! And believe me, you'll never know how rich that makes me feel. If God chooses to heal you in answer to prayer, that's great. Thank Him for it. But if He chooses not to, thank Him anyway. You can be sure He has His reasons. (136, 140–141, 155)

It is amazing to see the vast reservoir of hope that resides deep within the heart of Joni that she attributes directly to the trials resulting from her broken neck. She nowhere claims that God broke her neck. Rather she claims that God has used all involved in her broken neck for good (Romans 8:28).

Even though we may not be struggling with the level of difficulties that would come to us if we were paralyzed from the neck down, the problems we have can nevertheless begin to weigh heavily upon us. The trials of having several preschool children at home, the trials of not making enough money to easily meet the family's needs, the trials of not being appreciated at work or of being treated disrespectfully, the trials of being falsely accused of dishonorable things, the trials of poor health, the trials of broken relationships—all can be heavy trials.

Many such trials weigh heavily on us and can discourage us, tempting us to lose our hope. But in temptation, remember what our helmet is for. We must not look at the present circumstances, but instead cling to the hope of eternal salvation and the glory that is going to be ours.

The apostle Paul wrote of his own hope even in the face of remarkable trials. He said:

> We are hard-pressed on every side, yet not crushed; we are perplexed, but not in despair; persecuted, but not forsaken; struck down, but not destroyed—always carrying about in the body the dying of the Lord Jesus, that the life of Jesus also may be manifested in our body. (2 Corinthians 4:8–10)

More specifically Paul detailed what those trials were:

> From the Jews five times I received forty stripes minus one. Three times I was beaten with rods; once I was stoned; three times I was shipwrecked; a night and a day I have been in the deep; in journeys often, in perils of waters, in perils of robbers, in perils of my own countrymen, in perils of the Gentiles, in perils in the city, in perils in the wilderness, in perils in the sea, in perils among false brethren; in weariness and toil, in sleeplessness often, in hunger and thirst, in fastings often, in cold and nakedness—besides the other things, what comes upon me daily; my deep concern for all the churches. (2 Corinthians 11:24–28)

Paul had already written, however, that he knew that "He who raised up the Lord Jesus will also raise us up with Jesus, and will present us with you" (2 Corinthians 4:14). As a result of this certain hope of resurrection, he wrote:

> Therefore we do not lose heart. Even though our outward man is perishing, yet the inward man is being renewed day by day. For our light affliction, which is but for a moment, is working for us a far more exceeding and eternal weight of glory, while we do not look at the things which are seen, but at the things which are not seen. For the things which are seen are temporary, but the things which are not seen are eternal. (vv. 16–18)

When we look at the remarkable trials Paul endured as a Christian, it is incredible that he called them "light affliction." In Romans 8:18, we see him bouncing resolutely back from difficulties with the encouragement of his hope of heaven: "For I consider that the sufferings of this present time are not worthy to be compared with the glory that shall be revealed to us."

Paul's whole point: while he does not deny the sufferings of this life, he confidently emphasizes the glory that is going to be revealed to us. Again we see that biblical hope is all about the sure knowledge God deposits within us. Paul *knows* that future salvation shall come. This hope of the future completion of the salvation now in progress is the helmet protecting us in daily spiritual battle (Ephesians 1:13–14).

Future salvation will deliver us from the *presence* of sin.

If you would stand firm in the spiritual battle against the powers of darkness, the apostle Paul says, keep your mind fixed on your final and ultimate salvation. Put your heart in the next world while keeping your hands in this one. "Putting on . . . *as a helmet the hope of salvation.*"

HOW DO WE CULTIVATE AN ETERNAL PERSPECTIVE?

We cultivate an eternal perspective by viewing all temporal things in light of eternity.

Creation is groaning under the weight of sin (Romans 8:22–23), and we as human beings groan under its weight also.

On a global scale, we wish we could have peace. We wish that armies would not march against armies; that terrorists would not plant bombs and take hostages; that totalitarian governments would not oppress their own people.

But Scripture cautions us to expect wars and rumors of wars in this world—it warns of mankind's inhumanity to mankind. There will never be peace on earth. If we hope only in this world, we will be bitterly disappointed.

On a social scale, we wish we could have harmony. We wish we could end prejudice and bigotry, and corruption in government and business, and crime and abuse. We wish people would not destroy the environment and pollute the water and poison the air. We wish we could have a greater sense of community and be more willing to look out for each other.

But Scripture tells us to expect persecution and bigotry and selfishness and greed and crime and vice. Corrupt actions come from corrupt hearts.

On a personal level, we wish we could get people and possessions and circumstances to go the way we want them to; that our job could be as satisfying and pay us as much as we would like; that our kids would be mature and resist the pull of their peers. We wish we could lose weight on pizza and conquer illnesses with chocolate ice cream!

WHY I NEED TO KNOW ABOUT THIS

It is very difficult to live without hope. I must believe that there is something in the future worth pursuing, or I cannot go on in the present. The helmet of salvation gives me the hope I need to face the demands of the present and the uncertainties of life.

But Scripture teaches us that circumstances will fly up in our faces, that possessions will rust before our eyes, and that money will take wings and fly away. Solomon said that he had tried everything this world had to offer—fame, money, pleasure, achievement, alcohol—and none of it satisfied. It was like trying to bottle the wind or eat the sky. If we look to this world for satisfaction or fairness or healing, we will be continually disappointed.

Yet God does give us hope. For He says that this world is not all there is. This world is not our home; we are just passing through. We don't belong here any more than fish belong in the desert or camels belong in the sea. We belong to God. We are being fitted for heaven. That is our hope and our destination.

Joy. Satisfaction. Peace. Satisfying relationships. Anything pleasant and right and just and good is a mere foretaste of heaven. Anything harmful and bad and unjust and evil is a mere foretaste of hell, of eternity without God.

Live, then, for the next world. Put your hope in the promise of the next world. Change your values to the precepts of the next world. Develop your taste for the fruits of the next world. Do it, not because everything is bad in this world—it isn't—but because nothing in this world satisfies in the end, and nothing in this world offers permanent solution to anything.

HOW DO I TRANSFER MY HOPE FROM THIS WORLD TO THE NEXT?

I transfer my hope from this world to the next by using the disappointments of this world as a catalyst to consciously embrace God's answer to those disappointments.

What are you trusting in this life to give you meaning, joy, satisfaction, and peace?

If you are single, do you think getting married will give your life meaning? Without Christ, it won't.

If you are struggling financially, do you think more money will give you satisfaction? Without Christ, it won't.

If you are stuck in a dead-end job, do you think a career change will give you joy? Without Christ, it won't.

That doesn't mean you can't pursue these things if God gives you the freedom. Just don't expect them to give you the ultimate meaning, joy, satisfaction, and peace in life.

If you establish the foundation of your life on people, possessions, and circumstances, you will be kicked, scratched, beaten, and tripped. You will be hurt, disappointed, exhausted, and confused. Oh, things may go well occasionally, but eventually life spins out of control.

But if you get your basic, foundational meaning in life from God,

- if you get your longing for love met in the awareness that He, and He alone, can love you perfectly and unendingly;
- if you receive your feeling of significance from the fact that He has called you to the greatest cause of the ages, to know Him and make Him known;
- if you acquire your sense of purpose from the fact that He has gifted you to do certain things that only you can do, and that He wants to use you as a major player in His plan for the ages, both now and forever;
- then, the heartache and disappointment of life do not destroy you. You can truly enjoy the good things of life, as only the Christian who is walking closely with God can.

If you are depending on people, possessions, and circumstances to give your life significance and satisfaction, you will become confused, hurt, and angry with God when He doesn't give you the things you feel you need. But if you derive your significance and satisfaction from Him, then in good times *and* bad, life has meaning and purpose.

So, put on the helmet of the hope of salvation. Fix your mind, your hopes, your values on the world to come. The helmet will protect you from the deadly blows of the Enemy in this world.

SPEED BUMP!

Slow down long enough to be sure you've gotten the main points of this chapter.

Q1. What does the helmet of salvation picture?

A1. The helmet of salvation pictures a lifestyle of *hope* that comes from focusing on our ultimate salvation.

Q2. How do we cultivate an eternal perspective?

A1. We cultivate an eternal perspective by viewing all temporal things in light of *eternity.*

Q3. How do I transfer my hope from this world to the next?

A3. I transfer my hope from this world to the next by using the disappointments of this world as a catalyst to consciously *embrace* God's answer to those disappointments.

FILL IN THE BLANK

Q1. What does the helmet of salvation picture?

A1. The helmet of salvation pictures a lifestyle

of _____ that comes from focusing on our ultimate salvation.

Q2. How do we cultivate an eternal perspective?

A1. We cultivate an eternal perspective by viewing all temporal things in light of

_____.

Q3. How do I transfer my hope from this world to the next?

A3. I transfer my hope from this world to the next by using the disappointments of this world as a catalyst to consciously _____ God's answer to those disappointments.

FOR FURTHER THOUGHT AND DISCUSSION

1. Imagine that you have been visited by your own ghosts of Christmas past, present, and future. What might you learn from such a visit?

2. What are you aiming for in life that you believe will give you happiness? What if you don't get it? Will Jesus alone and what He chooses to give you be enough?

3. What is the most appealing thing about heaven that helps you put your hope in the next world?

WHAT IF I DON'T BELIEVE?

1. If I don't believe in the helmet of the hope of salvation, I lose the ability to interpret all temporal things in light of eternity.

2. I lose the ability to persevere through the difficulties of the present because I lose hope for the future.

3. I become discouraged and an easy target for the deception of Satan.

FOR FURTHER STUDY

1. Scripture

Several Scripture passages speak of the importance of righteousness:

- Romans 8:22–25
- 2 Corinthians 4:16–18
- Ephesians 6:17
- Colossians 3:1–2
- 1 Peter 1:13
- Romans 13:11–12
- 1 Thessalonians 5:8

Read these passages and consider how they add to your understanding of the importance of righteousness.

2. Books

Several other books are very helpful in studying this subject. They are listed below in general order of difficulty.

30 Days to Understanding How to Live as a Christian, Max Anders

Tramp for the Lord, Corrie ten Boom

Joy That Lasts, Gary Smalley

8

WHAT IS THE SWORD OF THE SPIRIT?

Defend the Bible? I would just as soon defend a lion. Just turn the Bible loose. It will defend itself.
—**Charles H. Spurgeon**

 t 7:00 P.M. on Monday night, April 14, 1986, thirteen fighter jets screamed in off the Mediterranean Ocean toward the Libyan city of Tripoli. Hurtling along near the speed of sound, no more than five hundred feet above the ground, these metal lightning bolts delivered their deadly cargo, then pulled up in a break-neck angle and turned back toward the Mediterranean and the safety of home base.

Later evaluation would show that every major target they had aimed for was hit: barracks, communication centers, a naval site, a terrorist headquarters, and on-ground planes and helicopters. President Reagan's retaliatory strike against Muammar al-Qadhafi's global terrorism was complete. Mission accomplished.

Hitting such small targets while traveling six hundred miles an hour only five hundred feet above the ground is like running down a steep hill as fast as you can and spitting on an anthill.

How did they do it? What made it possible?

Laser beams! Pencil-thin laser beams spotted the target electronically and then locked on to it with computer-controlled mechanisms. The bombs themselves also had a laser-sensing device that guided them to the targets.

Laser beam technology is revolutionizing warfare. President Reagan champi-oned his "Star Wars" initiative, which called for earth-orbiting satellites that would be able to direct laser beams onto incoming missiles and knock them out of the sky. Tanks, anti-aircraft guns, and even personal infantry weapons are being fitted with lasers to increase efficiency and minimize human error. Laser beams have a formi-dable future in modern warfare.

But laser beams are also a potent force for healing. At the fertility center at Northside Hospital in Atlanta, Dr. Cameron Nezhat guides a laser beam to remove endometriosis and increase a woman's chances for conception. In Colorado Springs, an ophthalmologist directs the tiny beam to tack a detached retina back in place for an Olympic athlete. At Roswell Park Memorial Institute in Buffalo, New York, Frank Rauscher reports that lasers are being used to destroy cancerous tumors, and many more highly advanced applications will appear as technology progresses.

Lasers (Light Amplification by Stimulated Emission of Radiation) produce an intense, penetrating beam of light that has awesome power both to destroy and to heal, to attack and to protect.

In the apostle Paul's day the weapon of both attack and protection was the soldier's sword.

WHAT DOES THE SWORD OF THE SPIRIT PICTURE?

The sword of the Spirit pictures an offensive and defensive use of the Bible in spiritual warfare.

And take . . . the sword of the Spirit, which is the word of God (Ephesians 6:17b).

The final piece of armor in the believer's arsenal is the sword of the Spirit. Different from the previous five pieces of armor, this sword is extremely powerful like the laser, and it has both an offensive and a defensive capacity.

The Roman soldier's sword (*machaira*) was short and double-bladed. This cut-and-thrust weapon, wielded by the heavily armed legionary, was distinct from the large Thracian broadsword (*rhomphaia*). The smaller Roman sword was used in hand-to-hand combat. A weapon of last resort, it was drawn in desperate, intense warfare.

The believer's sword is the Word of God. The Bible uses two different words for the Word of God. One is *logos*, which refers to the collection of words embodying the whole body of God's revealed truth. For us this is synonymous with the Bible. The second word, *rhema*, is the word used in this verse. *Rhema* often refers to specific, individual words. When we get involved in spiritual combat, we do not appeal to the entire Bible; we use specific, relevant passages—specific words of God.

For example, when you are tempted to get angry and really blow your top, it is not effective to say, "I believe the whole Bible." Instead, you counter temptation with, "The anger of man does not achieve the righteousness of God"; or, "A fool always loses his temper, / But a wise man holds it back"; or, "An angry man stirs up strife, / And a hot-tempered man abounds in transgression" (James 1:20; Proverbs 29:11, 22 NASB). The specific words of God are those that relate directly to the problem or temptation and thus help you be successful in the spiritual battle.

Commitment to the whole Bible is important in spiritual warfare, but this commitment occurs when we don the first piece of armor, the belt of truth. When we buckle on that belt, we accept the truth of the Bible and choose to follow it with integrity. Then, when we take up the sword of the Spirit, we use those Scriptures specifically in life's situations to fend off attacks of the Enemy and put him to flight.

But why does Paul call it the sword of the Spirit? Why doesn't he simply call it the sword of the Word? He calls it the sword of the Spirit for two reasons: first, because the Holy Spirit gave us the Word; and second, because the Holy Spirit helps us understand the Word.

Second Timothy 3:16 says, "All Scripture is given by inspiration of God." The word *inspired* means, literally, "God-breathed." And in 2 Peter 1:20–21 we are told that "no prophecy of Scripture is of any private interpretation, for prophecy never came by the will of man, but holy men of God spoke as they were moved by the Holy Spirit."

IN THIS CHAPTER WE LEARN THAT . . .

1. The sword of the Spirit pictures an offensive and defensive use of the Bible in spiritual warfare.

2. The sword is used defensively by applying Scripture to every doubt, temptation, and discouragement hurled at us by Satan.

3. The sword is used offensively to cause change, encouraging spiritual growth through evangelism, teaching, preaching, and counseling.

Theologians admit that we don't know exactly what this means, but somehow the Holy Spirit influenced the prophets and writers of Scripture to speak and write only what God wanted. Therefore, it is the Word of God.

So, the Word of God is called the sword of the Spirit because the Spirit of God gave it to us. Not surprisingly then, we need the Holy Spirit to help us understand it.

In the frustrating days just before I became a Christian, I tried reading the Bible, but I got nothing out of it. Defeated, I put it away. Months later I became a Christian, and suddenly I could not get enough of it. Not only did I want to read it, but I could understand it. I read and read and read and gradually understood more and more. I didn't understand everything (and still don't), but I understood some things, and I was content to read the Bible for what I *did* understand, rather than stop reading it because of what I *didn't* understand.

Mark Twain once said, "Many people are troubled by the things in the Scripture that they don't understand. Frankly, the ones that bother me are the ones that I do understand."

I can identify with that. I don't understand everything and never will. But what I do understand teaches me what I need to know about the Christian life and provides protection against the wiles of Satan.

HOW IS THE SWORD USED FOR DEFENSE?

The sword is used defensively by applying Scripture to every doubt,
temptation, and discouragement hurled at us by Satan.

All the pieces of the armor of God are closely linked to each other. For example, the defensive use of the sword of the Spirit is closely linked with the shield of faith. Every time we feel like doubting or sinning or quitting, we take up the shield to reject those thoughts, and tell ourselves the truth by brandishing the sword of the Spirit.

When Satan tempted Jesus with physical comfort, Jesus blocked that temptation with the shield of faith, calling it a lie. Then, He countered with the sword of the Spirit, telling the truth: "It is written, 'Man shall not live by bread alone, but by every word that proceeds from the mouth of God'" (Matthew 4:4). Jesus knew the specific portion of Scripture that addressed the temptation He was facing, and this defense gave Him the strength to overcome the Enemy.

When Satan tempted Jesus with power, Jesus knocked that temptation aside with the shield of faith and countered it with the sword of the Spirit: "Away with you, Satan! For it is written, 'You shall worship the LORD your God, and Him only you shall serve'" (v. 10).

Satan was vanquished in the battle because Jesus wielded the sword of the Spirit. The same protective armor is ours. Satan tempts. And because we know the Bible specifically, we can spot the error in what he is promising us and defend ourselves accordingly.

HOW IS THE SWORD USED FOR OFFENSE?

The sword is used offensively to cause change, encouraging spiritual
growth through evangelism, teaching, preaching, and counseling.

A teacher at Newton Massachusetts High School, one of the better high schools in the nation, quizzed a group of college-bound seniors before a "Bible as Literature" course he was planning to teach. From that quiz, according to the students' answers, he learned some astounding facts about the Bible: Sodom and Gomorrah were lovers; Jezebel was Ahab's donkey; the New Testament gospels were written by Matthew, Mark, Luther, and John; Eve was created from an apple; Jesus was baptized by Moses; and Golgotha was the name of the giant who slew the apostle David.

It's funny. But it's also sad. In the past, biblical knowledge was basic to American education. The great Ivy League schools of Harvard, Princeton, and Yale were founded primarily for the training of ministers of the Gospel. Today, however, our nation is increasingly ignorant of the Bible.

At the same time, our nation is being ravaged by broken homes, drug and alcohol abuse, physical and sexual abuse, runaway children and teenage pregnancies, venereal disease and AIDS in epidemic proportions, crime and graft in business and government, and illiteracy in a nation where education is compulsory. We are a nation in crisis.

Why? Because we do not know nor care to know the Bible. And sadly, even many Christians are woefully ignorant of God's Word.

We simply must learn the Bible. No matter how well we know it, we must get to know it better. A multitude of means to do this exist: Christian books and study guides, commentaries and other aids, Sunday school classes, home Bible studies, growth groups, community Bible studies, seminars, discipleship ministries—find the ways that work for you.

WHY I NEED TO KNOW THIS

The Bible is central to the Christian life, but most Christians do not know it well enough to apply it specifically to all the challenges and temptations of life. If Jesus, in Matthew 4:1–11, wielded the Scriptures very specifically to defeat the wiles of the devil in His life, so must we. Knowledge of the Scriptures is of paramount importance to our being victorious Christians, and we must commit ourselves to learning God's Word well enough to be effective in spiritual combat.

But remember, the Bible is not to be studied as an end in itself, but as a revelation of God and His truth to us so that our thinking, our values, our habits, our actions, our words, and most of all, our very lives are changed.

Change! That is the grand purpose of the Bible. Changing us so that we become more than the person we were yesterday, less like a fallen person and more like God.

God isn't merely a safety net or a lifeboat. He isn't just walking with us to rescue us from problems so that our lives will go smoother. He requires active participation from us. He demands our commitment, our allegiance, our worship, and our obedience. To do that, we need the power of the Word. "For the word of God is living and powerful, and sharper than any two-edged sword, piercing even to the division of soul and spirit, and of joints and marrow, and is a discerner of the thoughts and intents of the heart" (Hebrews 4:12).

When we learn the true Word and follow it,

hurting people are helped;
abused people are healed;
angry people are soothed;
depressed people are encouraged;
fearful people are given courage;
weak people are given strength;
confused people are given insight;
foolish people are given wisdom;
ignorant people are given knowledge;
selfish people are given generosity;
hateful people are given love;
doubting people are given faith;
aggressive people are given gentleness;
proud people are given humility.
It isn't quick and it isn't easy, but it is sure.

So take up the sword of the Spirit, which is the Word of God, and gain victory in the spiritual battles you face. Taking up the sword of the Spirit means that you will use the Scriptures specifically in life's situations to fend off attacks of the Enemy and put him to flight.

CONCLUSION

It is through the Bible that God makes known to humanity what He wants us to know. Hebrews 3:7 says, "Therefore, as the Holy Spirit says . . . ," and then it quotes a passage from an Old Testament psalm written by David. This is a striking passage because it attributes to God something that was written by a human being. It is apparent from this and other passages in the Bible that Scripture was *revealed* by God.

As we saw earlier, in 2 Timothy 3:16–17, all Scripture is *inspired* by God. Revelation means that God revealed His truth to the writers of the Scripture. Inspiration means that He worked through the process in such a way that that which He revealed was written down correctly.

The first and perhaps most important thing that can be said about the Bible, then, is that it clearly claims God as its author. Next we see that God empowers the Scripture. When the Bible is proclaimed, it accomplishes that which God intends. We read in Isaiah 55:11, "So shall My word be that goes forth from My mouth; it shall not return to Me void, but it shall accomplish what I please, and it shall prosper *in the thing* for which I sent it" (emphasis added).

Also supporting the power of the Scripture, in a beautifully poetic passage penned by David, the king of Israel, we read:

> The law of the LORD is perfect,
>   converting the soul;
> The testimony of the LORD is sure,
>   making wise the simple;
> The statutes of the LORD are right,
>   rejoicing the heart;
> The commandment of the LORD is pure,
>   enlightening the eyes;
> The fear of the LORD is clean,
>   enduring forever;
> The judgments of the LORD are true
>   and righteous altogether.
> More to be desired are they than gold,
> Yea, than much fine gold;
> Sweeter also than honey and the
>   honeycomb.
> Moreover by them Your servant is
>   warned,
> And in keeping them there is great
>   reward. (Psalm 19:7–11)

What a powerful testimony to the power of Scripture. We see that God's Word will convert the soul, make wise the simple, rejoice the heart, enlighten the eyes, and endure forever, and that it is more to be desired than gold. It is sweeter than honey, and by reading the Scripture the servant of God is warned and in keeping the Scripture there is great reward.

The Bible is able to transfer people from the kingdom of darkness into the kingdom of light as they follow its teachings and commit their lives to Christ. It can move them from living in the realm of sin and death to living in the realm of righteousness and life. It can change sadness into joy, despair into hope, foolishness into wisdom, and failure into success.

It is because the Word of God is so powerful and effective in people's lives that Satan works so hard to neutralize its influence in the lives of Christians. He will do whatever he can to undermine God's Word to those who hear it. Jesus told the parable of the sower in which He pictured Satan as ready to snatch God's Word from the hearer's heart before it had a chance to take root (Matthew 13:19). Whenever we give ourselves in faithful obedience to studying and living the truth of the Scripture, we find our lives dramatically changed.

D. Martin Lloyd Jones was the pastor of a large church in England for many years and developed a worldwide reputation as a profound expositor of the Scripture. In his book *The Christian Soldier*, he wrote,

> Luther was held in darkness by the devil, though he was a monk. He was trying to save himself by works. He was fasting, sweating, and praying; and yet he was miserable and unhappy, and in bondage. Superstitious Roman Catholic teaching held him captive. But he was delivered by the Word of God—"the just shall live by faith." From that moment he began to understand this Word as he had never understood it before, and the better he understood it, the more he saw the errors taught by Rome. He saw the error of her practice, and so became more intent on the reformation of the church. He proceeded to do all in terms of exposition of the scriptures. The great doctors in the Roman church stood against him. He sometimes had to stand alone and meet them in close combat, and invariably he took his stand upon the scripture. He maintained that the church is not above the scriptures. The standard by which you judge even the church, he said, is the scripture. And though he was one man at first standing alone, he was able to fight the papal system and twelve centuries of tradition. He did so by taking up "the sword of the spirit, which is the Word of God." (331)

As we saw earlier, in Matthew 4 and Luke 4 in the accounts of His temptation by Satan, each time Satan tempted Him, Jesus quoted Scripture in response. If Jesus found the Scripture so powerful and used it so effectively, if saints of old have found Scripture so powerful and used it so effectively, if mature Christians all around us find Scripture so powerful and use it so effectively, could we expect to live a victorious Christian life without also founding our lives on the sword of the Spirit?

SPEED BUMP!

Slow down long enough to make sure you've gotten the main points of this chapter.

Q1. What does the sword of the Spirit picture?

A1. The sword of the Spirit pictures an offensive and defensive use of the *Bible* in spiritual warfare.

Q2. How is the sword used for defense?

A2. The sword is used *defensively* by applying Scripture to every doubt, temptation, and discouragement hurled at us by Satan.

Q3. How is the sword used for offense?

A3. The sword is used *offensively* to cause change, encouraging spiritual growth through evangelism, teaching, preaching, and counseling.

FILL IN THE BLANK

Q1. What does the sword of the Spirit picture?

A1. The sword of the Spirit pictures an offensive and defensive use of the _____ in spiritual warfare.

Q2. How is the sword used for defense?

A2. The sword is used _____ by applying Scripture to every doubt, temptation, and discouragement hurled at us by Satan.

Q3. How is the sword used for offense?

A3. The sword is used _____ to cause change, encouraging spiritual growth through evangelism, teaching, preaching, and counseling.

FOR FURTHER THOUGHT AND DISCUSSION

1. The Bible, like a laser beam, can be used for defensive or offensive purposes. Jesus quoted Scripture to Satan in answer to his temptations. What subject would you like to know more about to be able to use that truth to defend yourself against temptation? How will you pursue that information?

2. What pain in the world do you wish you could help alleviate? How could you learn more about the Bible in that area?

3. In what area of your life would you like to experience the most change? What first step could you take toward that end—after praying about it?

WHAT IF I DON'T BELIEVE?

1. If I don't believe in the importance of the Scripture in spiritual warfare, I will not be as diligent a student of the Scripture as I need to be to successfully defend myself against the wiles of the devil.

2. I will not have the level of respect for the written Word of God, which was sanctioned by Jesus Himself, that I need to have.

3. I will not have answers to give to others under spiritual attack.

4. I become susceptible to the deception of Satan and ineffective in advancing into his territory to gain spiritual victories in my life and the lives of those to whom I minister.

FOR FURTHER STUDY

1. Scripture

Several Scripture passages speak of the importance of righteousness:

- John 1:1
- Ephesians 6:17
- 2 Timothy 3:16–17
- Hebrews 4:12
- Revelation 19:13

Read these passages and consider how they add to your understanding of the importance of the sword of the Spirit.

2. Books

Several other books are very helpful in studying this subject. They are listed below in general order of difficulty.

30 Days to Understanding How to Live as a Christian, Max Anders
30 Days to Understanding What Christians Believe, Max Anders
The Bible: Embracing God's Truth, Max Anders
God Has Spoken, James I. Packer

9

We cannot all argue, but we can all pray; we cannot all be leaders, but we can all be pleaders; we cannot all be mighty in rhetoric, but we can all be prevalent in prayer. I would sooner see you eloquent with God than with men.
—**Charles H. Spurgeon**

WHAT ROLE DOES PRAYER PLAY IN SPIRITUAL WARFARE?

During the Civil War, two Quaker ladies were discussing the relative merits and prospects of Abraham Lincoln and Jefferson Davis.

"I think Jefferson will succeed because he is a praying man," said one.

"But so is Abraham a praying man," said the other.

"Yes," rejoined the first lady, "but the Lord will think that Abraham is joking."

While Abraham Lincoln told this humorous story on himself many times, it may strike a responsive chord in many of us; for many have the nagging suspicion that when they pray, the Lord thinks they are joking. The reality is, many of us are uneasy about prayer. To one degree or another we feel unworthy and inadequate. We're not sure if we are qualified to pray. We're not even sure we know how to pray.

On the other hand, we all feel pulled to pray. Even those who say they are not very religious or those who have never made a commitment to Christ instinctively find themselves thanking the Lord for good things and—especially—calling on Him in times of trouble.

As believers, we see the inherent virtue in prayer and wish we were better at it. Created by God for fellowship with Him, without prayer we sense a void. God is calling us. Nothing else will satisfy. We want to draw near to God and have Him draw near to us (James 4:8).

Paul tells us in Ephesians 6 that if we want to be victorious in spiritual warfare, we must obey six biblical principles pictured as six pieces of armor. Then he follows these principles with a summary principle: pray.

HOW DO WE MAKE CONTACT
WITH OUR COMMANDER?

In the spiritual war, we make contact with our Commander through prayer.

With all prayer and petition pray at all times in the Spirit, and with this in view, be on the alert with all perseverance and petition for all the saints (Ephesians 6:18 NASB).

Paul gives us four "alls" to guide us in understanding his instructions on prayer:

1. with all prayer and petition—the scope of prayer
2. at all times in the Spirit—the attitude of prayer
3. with all perseverance and petition—the fervency of prayer
4. for all the saints—the target of prayer.

The Scope of Prayer. Prayer comes from the word *proseuché*, which refers to general requests, while petition comes from *deésis*, referring to specific requests. This includes thanks and praise to God, confession of sin, pouring out to God the thoughts and feelings of our mind and heart, general prayer for things on our minds, and requests for specific things that concern us.

The Attitude of Prayer. Praying at all times does not mean that we walk around with our hands folded or that we spend all our time on our knees. Rather, we should be in an attitude of prayer through the whole day. Praying in the Spirit means that we do not recite meaningless prayers but that we depend on God's guidance in what we pray for. It means recognizing and depending upon the fact stated in Romans 8:26–27: "For we do not know what we should pray for as we ought, but the Spirit Himself makes intercession for us with groanings which cannot be uttered. Now He who searches the hearts knows what the mind of the Spirit is, because He makes intercession for the saints according to the will of God." Praying at all times in the Spirit means we have an attitude of submission to, dependence on, and guidance from the Holy Spirit in our praying.

> **Prayer is our spiritual supply line.**

The Fervency of Prayer. Fervency doesn't mean that we have to work ourselves up to a fever pitch every time we pray. Rather, Paul is reflecting Jesus' teaching on prayer and the principle of perseverance in our petitions (Luke 18:2–7).

The Target of Prayer. We are members of the body of Christ; therefore, what other Christians are doing is of interest to us. When Billy Graham preaches in a crusade, when Christian leaders gather in the Philippines for a conference on world evangelization, when friends, missionaries, and ministry leaders are involved in ministry and outreach, their activities are important to us. And we should pray for them.

Based on this teaching, Paul appeals to the Ephesian church to pray for him. But notice his request. He doesn't ask for material things. He asks that he may be given boldness in witnessing.

Left to themselves, the Ephesians might have prayed—as would we—that he be released from prison. They might have prayed that God would give him health. They might have prayed that God would comfort him and allow him to be freed to go back to Jerusalem to live a normal life.

But Paul did not want that. He had accepted his circumstances as being from God and said, "Pray that I might be an effective witness for the cause of Christ. That is why I am here."

HOW DO WE GET A RESPONSE FROM OUR COMMANDER?

We get a response from our Commander by praying according to the guidelines given us in Scripture.

In an old *Peanuts* cartoon I saw many years ago, Linus is looking quizzically at his folded hands. Lucy comes up, and Linus says, "I have just made an important theological discovery. I have discovered that while you are praying, if you hold your hands upside down, you get the opposite of what you pray for."

Many of us have suspected that all along. We have been holding our hands upside down and are getting just the opposite of what we are asking for!

We don't know and understand a lot of things about prayer, but we must not let that keep us from praying. We must not let the things we don't understand destroy the things we do.

First of all, we must understand that God wants us to pray. He is waiting for us to pray—not in the same way that the IRS with hands on hips and ready to box our ears wants and waits for us to file our income tax—but like a loving parent wanting and waiting to hear His child's

IN THIS CHAPTER WE LEARN THAT . . .

1. In the spiritual war, we make contact with our Commander through prayer.

2. We get a response from our Commander by praying according to the guidelines given us in Scripture.

3. We foster a relationship with our Commander because our relationship with God is even more important than a specific answer to a given prayer.

requests, with an earnest desire to answer. God does answer our prayers. God does not grant all our requests; however, He will answer *those that are answerable.*

Now, I can hear you shouting at me, "But how do I know which ones are answerable?"

Well, we can't get too detailed in answering this, but there seem to be several levels of restriction on receiving answers to prayer. One verse says, simply, that we should ask and we will receive (Matthew 7:8). Period. No qualifications. Taken in isolation, this verse seems to indicate that no request will be denied us.

However, other verses add qualifications to our asking. For example, James 1:6 says that we must "ask in faith, with no doubting." John 14:13 admonishes us to ask in Jesus' name. Psalm 66:18 says, "If I regard iniquity in my heart, the LORD will not hear." And in John 15:7 we learn that we must abide in Him and His Word must abide in us, and *then* we can ask what we will and it will be given to us. Finally, we see that Jesus prayed in the Garden of Gethsemane just before His crucifixion, "Your will be done" (Matthew 26:42). So, it seems that when we put all the verses on prayer together, we can observe levels of restrictions on prayer:

Level 1: Ask and you shall receive—no qualifications.
Level 2: Ask in faith, without doubting; ask without unconfessed sin—specific qualifications.
Level 3: Abide in Me and My Word in you—general qualification.
Level 4: Thy will be done—final qualification.

Although not exhaustive, this summary suggests a checklist with which we might analyze our prayers.

First, we are given the open invitation to simply ask. If we do not receive an answer, we may check ourselves on level 2. Are we asking in faith? Do we have any unconfessed sin that could be hindering the answer? Does the request conflict with anything in the Bible that would indicate that the request is not in God's will? Are we asking with proper motives?

> Proper motives are prerequisites to effectual prayer.

If that level seems to check out, then we may need to move on to level 3, where we check on our overall spiritual maturity. Are we abiding in Christ, and is His Word abiding in us? Perhaps God is delaying the answer to prayer because He wants to draw us into a deeper walk with Him.

If we gain no insight or receive no answer on this level, we move to level 4, where we simply pray, "Thy will be done." This is, of course, the prayer Jesus prayed in the

Garden of Gethsemane when He asked that the Father would take this cup (being crucified) from Him but then said, "Nevertheless not my will, but thine be done" (Luke 22:42 KJV).

In reality, of course, we do not compartmentalize our prayers to this degree. However, we ought to make a simultaneous check of all these things as we are praying. Analyzing them this way helps us see if we have overlooked possible hindrances within ourselves to God's answering our prayers.

Sometimes God simply delays the answers to our prayers. Why? Well, there may be several reasons:

- The timing is not right. He may answer it—later.
- The request may need to be clarified. When the answer comes, God wants us to be able to recognize it. Often we don't recognize an answer because we did not crystallize the request in our own minds.
- God might want to intensify our expectations and to call attention to the fact that it was He who answered, not just good luck or natural consequences.
- He wants to deepen our understanding of Him and His Word.
- He is drawing us into a deeper relationship with Him. Things that come easily are often taken lightly. God does not want prayer to be taken lightly. Therefore, answers to prayer do not always come readily.

WHY DO WE FOSTER A RELATIONSHIP WITH OUR COMMANDER?

We foster a relationship with our Commander because our relationship with God is even more important than a specific answer to a given prayer.

The relationship between parent and child gives us great insight into the relationship between our heavenly Father and us, His children. When a child is young, uneducated, and immature, he often asks for silly things, even dangerous things. He wants to have only candy for lunch; he wants to drive the car and run the vacuum; he loves to walk down the middle of the street. The loving and perceptive parent would surely not grant all the requests of a two-year-old.

As the child grows older, his requests become less ridiculous and impossible. His whole life falls more into line with the parent's will. Yet even when the child reaches the teenage years, parents cannot grant all their child's requests. Some are still foolish; others are selfish and manipulative.

Grown into enlightened adulthood, the child makes few requests that a parent cannot grant, because they are asked with a knowledge and understanding consistent with the parent's will. And the adult child understands—especially if he has children of his own—that his parents did not refuse childhood requests because they didn't love him. Their denial of the request was rooted in their greater knowledge and wisdom.

God is not Cosmic Customer Service where every order will be filled as requested, so long as the form is filled out properly. Let us envision Him as He really is—our heavenly Father who loves us and wants the best for us in all His sovereign wisdom and who answers or doesn't answer based on His superior, all-knowing will. This correct vision of God keeps us through times when we experience a sense of failure or doubt or disappointment when our prayers aren't answered in just the way and at the time we prescribe.

If we approach God with this understanding, rather than eyeing Him as some Heavenly Vending Machine we are tempted to shake or kick when it doesn't give us what we want ("What in the world is *wrong* with this thing?"), we can say to God as we want maturing children to say to a loving parent, "Well, I guess that request is not what is best for me right now. I will accept the refusal."

> God yearns for us to develop a relationship with Him.

The bottom line in prayer is that God wants a relationship with us. That is His ultimate desire. So He refuses any approach that will allow us simply to work through an equation to get what we want. Formulas won't work. The only thing that will work is personally drawing closer to Him. As we do, our requests may change as we conform more and more to His priorities and purposes.

That is why no one fully understands prayer in a way that can be communicated to others as a *system*. There is a very personal and intimate dimension to prayer: there is no system. It is you and God alone in a room, both wanting what is best for you, and your learning to trust and follow Him. Only by getting to know Him better will prayer begin to make sense.

WHY I NEED TO KNOW THIS

If it is true that we can be strong only *in the Lord* (Ephesians 6:10), then He, not some technique or equation, is our strength in the spiritual war. Therefore, fellowship with Him is of paramount importance. It is He who protects us, guides us, and empowers us. Therefore, we would be extremely foolish if we attempted to wage war in our own strength.

So pray! Risk praying poorly. Pray the best way you know how. Don't allow that which you don't understand about prayer keep you from praying. And do not let that which you don't understand about prayer destroy that which you do understand. *Pray!* God will lead you into fuller understanding over time.

Remember:

- We can pray to God because Christ has made us acceptable to Him. We are completely free to enter the Most Holy Place (a metaphor for worshiping and praying directly to God) without fear because of the sacrifice of Jesus' blood and body that opens access that will never be denied (Hebrews 10:19–22). So we can come to God with a sincere heart and a sure faith, for we have been cleansed and made free from guilt.
- Because God knows everything, we can be completely and utterly honest before Him and know that we will be accepted, understood, and helped.
- When we hurt, God hurts. Therefore, we cannot accuse Him of not caring or of being distant when our prayers for relief are not answered.
- To pray effectively, we must know God's will. To learn His will, we must know His Word and be obedient to it.
- Gratitude should be our attitude in prayer for all that God does for us.
- Learning to pray well takes time.

CONCLUSION

I've often been amazed by how dogs absolutely love to do that for which they were bred. Bird dogs love to hunt birds. Put them in the truck and start driving toward the fields, and they quiver with excitement. Sled dogs live to pull sleds. They bark and howl in anticipation as they are hitched to the traces. And when the whip cracks and they hear their master shout, "Mush!" their ecstasy is undisguised. When these dogs do what they are created to do, they are filled with joy.

And so it is with us. God created us for fellowship with Him. When we commune with Him in prayer, a deep joy and satisfaction that nothing else can duplicate result from it. Prayer is our direct source and hookup to His power. It is our access to His guidance and peace. It is a longing nothing else will satisfy. Few have said it as well as that great preacher from the nineteenth century, Charles Haddon Spurgeon:

> Prayer is the lisping of the believing infant, the shout of the fighting believer, the requiem of the dying saint falling asleep in Jesus. It is the breath, the watchword, the comfort, the strength, and the honor of a Christian. (*Morning and Evening*, January 2, Morning)

God created us for eternity with Him, which is where our inheritance and our riches are stored. Thus, in this never-enough world we must always remember who we really are and where our true wealth, purpose, love, and power really lie.

Ray Stedman, well-known and beloved pastor, knew this well. A year before his death in 1992, he preached these words:

> The world tells us, if you don't take it now, you're never going to get another chance. I have seen that misunderstanding drive people into forsaking their marriages after 30 or 40 years and running off with another, usually younger, person, hoping they can still fulfill their dreams because they feel life is slipping away from them. Christians are not to think that way. This life is a school, a training period where we are being prepared for something that is incredibly great but is yet to come. I don't understand all that is involved in that, but I believe it, and sometimes I can hardly wait until it happens. Don't succumb to the philosophy that you have to have it all now or you will never have another chance. You can pass by a lot of things now and be content because you know that what God is sending you now is just what you need to get you ready for what he has waiting for you when this life is over. ("Ready for Something Tremendous!" 11. Used by permission.)

SPEED BUMP!

Slow down long enough to be sure you've gotten the main points of this chapter.

Q1. How do we make contact with our Commander?

A1. In the spiritual war, we make contact with our Commander through *prayer*.

Q2. How do we get a response from our Commander?

A2. We get a response from our Commander by praying according to the *guidelines* given us in Scripture.

Q3. Why do we foster a relationship with our Commander?

A3. We foster a relationship with our Commander because our *relationship* with God is even more important than a specific answer to a given prayer.

FILL IN THE BLANK

Q1. How do we make contact with our Commander?

A1. In the spiritual war, we make contact with our Commander through

_____.

Q2. How do we get a response from our Commander?

A2. We get a response from our Commander by praying according to the
_____ given us in Scripture.

Q3. Why do we foster a relationship with our Commander?

A3. We foster a relationship with our Commander because our _____
with God is even more important than a specific answer to a given prayer.

FOR FURTHER THOUGHT AND DISCUSSION

1. Are there any prayers you have prayed that God did not answer? If so, are you
now glad that He didn't? What does that tell you about future prayers?

2. What would life be like if God always answered everyone's prayers?

3. How important is prayer in your life? When, why, and how do you pray? What
does this tell you?

WHAT IF I DON'T BELIEVE?

1. I will feel all alone, with the impression that I am going through life by myself.

2. I will be powerless and directionless in the spiritual war.

3. I will be susceptible to Satan's deceptions.

FOR FURTHER STUDY

1. Scripture

Several Scripture passages speak of the importance of prayer:

- Luke 11:1
- Romans 12:12
- Ephesians 6:18
- Philippians 4:6–7
- 1 Thessalonians 5:17

Read these passages and consider how they add to your understanding of the importance of prayer.

2. Books

Several other books are very helpful in studying this subject. They are listed below in general order of difficulty.

30 Days to Understanding How to Live as a Christian, Max Anders (especially chapter 23)

Too Busy Not to Pray, Bill Hybels

Growing in Christ, James I. Packer

10

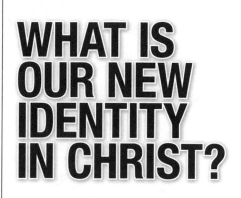

WHAT IS OUR NEW IDENTITY IN CHRIST?

We are half-hearted creatures, fooling about with drink and sex and ambition, when infinite joy is offered us, like an ignorant child who wants to go on making mud pies in a slum because he cannot imagine what is meant by the offer of a holiday at sea. We are far too easily pleased.
—**C. S. Lewis**

People spend a fortune today trying to discover who they are. They get color coordinated on the outside and psychoanalyzed on the inside. Tracing back to their earliest memories and beyond, they search for self-identity. This is not surprising, of course. It is the natural longing of the human heart, the seeking of the human soul after God. We long to know who we really are!

This is true for us even as Christians. We do not understand who we are and who we have become. We do not see ourselves as God sees us. Instead of accepting and comprehending who we have become in Christ, we identify with the person we used to be. So we must be imprinted with the proper identity. Otherwise, we'll be like the duck who thought he was a dog.

Sounds like a Disney cartoon or a Dr. Seuss story, doesn't it? But it is nothing so fanciful. Imprinting happens in real life.

Imprinting. The dictionary defines it as "a rapid learning process that takes place early in the life of a social animal and establishes a behavior pattern as recognition of and attraction to its own kind or a substitute." Ducks, for example, attach themselves to the first thing they see after they hatch. Normally this works just fine because the first thing they usually see is Mama Duck. They attach themselves to her and begin thinking and acting like her. This is fine. They are like her. They are ducks.

Occasionally this early attachment backfires, however, such as the duckling that hatched under the watchful eye of a collie dog. The first thing the baby duck saw was the collie, and a bond was forged. The duckling took one look at the collie and decided that it, too, was a collie. It followed the dog around, ran to it for protection, spent the hot part of the day under the porch with the collie, and slept with it at night. After the duckling grew up, it usually acted like a duck except for its spending the hot part of the day under the front porch. And when a car pulled into the driveway, the duck would explode from wherever it happened to be, quacking viciously and pecking at the tires. After all, that was what the "other" dog did.

The duck had an identity problem. It didn't see itself as a duck; it saw itself as a collie. Yet that couldn't change the fact that it was a duck. So sometimes it acted like a duck, and sometimes it acted like a dog.

This type of confusion is seen even more dramatically in the cases of children who have been reared by wild animals. During the last several hundred years there have been fifty-three documented cases of "feral children"; that is, children who have been lost in the wild and have survived by being nurtured, protected, and cared for by wild animals such as wolves, bears, antelopes, monkeys, and pigs.

Imprinting establishes identity.

The January/February 1987 edition of *Sierra* magazine told a story of "Uganda's Wild Child," a "monkey child" who was found in a jungle in Uganda and was believed to have been living with a tribe of monkeys for as long as four or five years. The boy, estimated to be five or six years old at the time, was taken to an orphanage, where he grunted and squealed, jumped around with his hands clenched, and preferred to eat grass. He seemed to be afraid of people and tried to scratch anyone who approached him.

Another example was a boy who had somehow become part of an antelope herd in southern Morocco. "Antelope boy" lived with the antelope, ate grass with them, drank from the same pools of water, and ran with them. Several attempts were made to capture him, to no avail, and he was observed living in this natural habitat over a period of ten years.

Those who have studied these wild children have determined that if a child lives with animals beyond the age of four to six years, he cannot be reclaimed as a normal-functioning human. These children are imprinted, their brains impressed indelibly and permanently with animal behavior; they lose their human identity. They do not understand that they are human, not animal. And the results are tragic.

While these are extreme and bizarre examples, a similar thing has happened with us. The Bible teaches that we have all been born flawed with sin. Theologians call it "total depravity." This doesn't mean that we cannot do good, but that we cannot keep from doing bad. Because of this sin we are born with, we are separated from God, and cannot correct the situation ourselves. Only God can. He offers salvation by grace through faith in Jesus Christ (Ephesians 2:8–9). When we believe in Jesus and receive Him as our Savior (John 1:12), we are born again (John 3:6–7). We become children of God. We are no longer what we were. The Bible announces, "If anyone is in Christ, he is a new creation; old things have passed away; behold, all things have become new" (2 Corinthians 5:17).

Even with that, however, we suffer from a kind of negative spiritual imprinting. We have all grown up in a fallen world, and the attitudes, values, and habits that we see in the world, we tend to embrace ourselves. These old patterns of thinking exert a lingering force over us, even as new creations in Christ. As a result, too often, we don't see ourselves as new creations. We are influenced more than necessary to continue thinking and feeling and acting as we did before we became Christians. The world, the flesh, and the devil play on our old ways of thinking, deceiving us into continuing to act like who we were before we came to Christ, holding us back from living out our new life in Christ. We are ducks acting like dogs. Instead of swimming around in clear, blue lakes, bobbing for seaweed, and preening our feathers, we are quacking at cars or harassing the cat.

HOW DOES GOD SEE US?

God sees us in Christ, having been born again in righteousness and true holiness in spirit, awaiting our complete adoption, the redemption of our bodies.

Fortunately, we are not permanently imprinted like the duck or the monkey child. We can be changed. We can begin to act more consistently with our true identity. God has promised to change the willing mind and to work supernaturally from within us to accomplish change (Philippians 2:12–13). In fact, that's our biggest challenge as believers.

So how do we find our true identity? We begin by seeing ourselves as God sees us, and in his letter to the Ephesians, the apostle Paul helps us with that. Notice how Paul addresses these ordinary Christians—people like you and me. He calls these ordinary Christians "saints": "Paul, an apostle of Christ Jesus by the will of God, to the *saints* who are in Ephesus, and faithful in Christ Jesus" (Ephesians 1:1, emphasis added).

All Christians are saints, in the biblical sense of the word. "Saint" comes from the Greek word *hagios*, which means "set apart for God." It does not necessarily mean a saintly lifestyle, such as that of Mother Teresa. It simply means that any Christian, anyone who has believed in and received Christ as his or her personal Savior, is a saint. If you are a Christian—if you believe in Christ and have committed your life to Him—you are set apart for God. You are *hagios*. You are a saint, and what the Lord says to the Ephesian believers through Paul, He says to you!

What, then, does Paul say to the Ephesian believers? Well, first of all, he uses a phrase that is so important that he uses it and related phrases twenty-seven times in his letter. The phrase is "in Christ." And if we are going to understand how God sees us, we must understand what it means to be "in Christ."

That's not always easy with our finite minds, so an analogy might help. For example, substitute the word *Congress* for "Christ." If you were a senator or a repre-sentative, we would say that you were "in Congress." What would that mean?

> **We must understand what being "in Christ" means.**

Well, if you are "in Congress," you have been elected to that position with due process of law. All the power, privi-leges, and responsibilities of that position are yours. You are a member of Congress. You have a place there. You are accepted there. You got there through required means, so you are wor-thy to be there. When you walk into the congressional cham-bers, no heads jerk up in surprise. Nobody says, "What are you doing here?" Why? Because you belong there.

To be "in Christ" means you belong in Christ. You have been elected by God. All the power, privileges, and responsibilities of that position are yours. You are a mem-ber of His body. You have a place there. You are accepted there.

You got there through required means (the kindness of God expressed through Christ), so you are worthy to be there. When you walk into heaven, no heads will jerk up in surprise. Nobody will say, "What are you doing here?" Why? Because you belong there.

Since we are dealing with infinite things, however, we must move beyond this finite analogy. For while there is no mystery about Congress—well, none except how they ever manage to get anything done—something about the spiritual is always just a bit beyond our natural understanding. And while a member of Congress is only as secure as the next election, being "in Christ" means that everything that is His is ours forever. Jesus never has to be reelected. Just as He is holy and righteous, so we are holy and righteous in Him. All His holiness, righteousness, goodness, glory, power, and wealth are ours!

"But wait," you say. "Something is wrong here. I don't feel holy, righteous, good, glorious, powerful, or wealthy. In fact, just between you and me, I'm not always good. I do some ugly things. I'm selfish. And sometimes I know what I'm doing is wrong, but I do it anyway. What you are saying may be true for other Christians, but it's not true for me. There's something wrong with me."

I know how you feel. If you were a fish, you'd be under the limit; you'd have to be thrown back. If you were a car, you'd be recalled.

This negative, there-must-be-something-wrong-with-me feeling is common among Christians. But central to understanding what it means to be in Christ, central to overcoming the negative spiritual imprinting of the world and identifying with who we really are is this understanding: we are *in Christ.*

That means God sees us through Christ's righteousness. Satisfied with Christ, He thus is satisfied with us because we are in Christ. Once we have

> **IN THIS CHAPTER WE LEARN THAT . . .**
>
> 1. God see us in Christ, having been born again in righteousness and true holiness in spirit, awaiting our complete adoption, the redemption of our bodies.
> 2. Our response should be gratitude and obedience.

accepted His offer of salvation, our identity no longer depends on who we are; it depends on who He is. We are secure in God's love because our being in Christ is

His will, not ours (Ephesians 1:5)
His grace, not ours (Ephesians 1:6–7)
His good pleasure, not ours (Ephesians 1:9)
His purpose, not ours (Ephesians 1:11)
His power, not ours (Ephesians 1:12, 14)
His calling, not ours (Ephesians 1:18)
His inheritance, not ours (Ephesians 1:18)
His love, not ours (Ephesians 2:4)
His workmanship, not ours (Ephesians 2:10).

"But I don't deserve it," you say. And if you are referring to personal merit, you are right. You don't deserve it. The Scriptures tell us that what we deserve is hell, eternal separation from the God against whom we have rebelled. But they also tell us that God chooses to value us greatly. God loves us so much that He sent that which was most precious to Him—His only Son, Jesus—to receive what we deserved by His dying for us. Because God freely chose to value us so greatly, we may trust His evaluation of us as valuable—created in His image and created again by new birth for new life in Christ.

Once we begin to get an accurate picture of who we really are and how God really sees us, light begins dawning in our darkened understanding. Then we try to live up to our image by acting more consistently like who we have actually become. This realization prompts us to behave more like God and less like the world. Our guarantee of this astounding truth is that phrase "in Christ."

What Christ has, we have. We are "fellow heirs" with Him (Romans 8:17 NASB). He is not ashamed to call us brothers and sisters (Hebrews 2:11). What Christ possesses, we possess: an imperishable and undefiled inheritance that will not fade away, reserved in heaven for us (1 Peter 1:4). And God has "blessed us with every spiritual blessing in the heavenly places in Christ" (Ephesians 1:3).

> When we see ourselves as God sees us in Christ, we can relax and *enjoy* God.

Now, you may be saying at this point, "I don't feel all that blessed." I used to feel that way. I thought that as a Christian I ought to have a continuous sense of being blessed, but I wasn't even sure what those blessings were! I have learned, however, that Paul did not leave that to our imagination. He enumerated our spiritual blessings in Christ in the next several verses of Ephesians chapter 1:

- He chose us to be holy and blameless (1:4).
- He predestined us to adoption (1:5).
- He freely bestowed His grace on us (1:6).
- He redeemed us and forgave our trespasses (1:7).
- He gave us an inheritance (1:11).

To gain a more personal sense of what this means to us, read these same truths as personal affirmations.

- I am chosen by God.
- I am holy and blameless before Him.
- I am adopted through His Son.
- I am a recipient of His grace, His generous kindness.
- I am redeemed.
- I am forgiven of all my sins.
- I have been given an inheritance.

WHAT SHOULD OUR RESPONSE BE TO OUR NEW IDENTITY IN CHRIST?

Our response should be gratitude and obedience.

Everything God asks of us is for our good. So when we are tempted to be dishonest or unethical or immoral or lazy or selfish, God says, "Don't do it! It will only hurt you! Remember who you are. Remember your identity. You do not belong in the world anymore. You are in Christ. Don't do these things just for My sake, but for yours! I hate sin because I love you! And sin hurts you."

When we understand who we are, we start acting like who we are, not who we were. And when we see ourselves as God sees us in Christ, we can relax and enjoy God. Certainly there is still work to be done, responsibilities to be assumed, reverence to be maintained. But as the Westminster Catechism reminds us, "Man's chief end is to glorify God and to enjoy Him forever." Not until we enjoy God have we entered into the fullness of what He wants to give us in Christ.

In *Desiring God*, John Piper wrote:

> **WHY I NEED TO KNOW THIS**
>
> We all tend to act consistently with how we see ourselves. If we have too low a view of ourselves, we are apt not to live up to the expectations God has for us. We then underestimate what God might be willing to do in us and through us.

1. The longing to be happy is a universal human experience, and it is good, not sinful.

2. We should never try to deny or resist our longing to be happy, as though it were a bad impulse. Instead we should seek to intensify this longing and nourish it with whatever will provide the deepest and most enduring satisfaction.

3. The deepest and most enduring happiness is found only in God.

4. The happiness we find in God reaches its consummation when it is shared with others in the manifold ways of love.

5. To the extent we try to abandon the pursuit of our own pleasure, we fail to honor God and love people. Or, to put it positively: the pursuit of pleasure is a necessary part of all worship and virtue. That is: The chief end of man is to glorify God by enjoying Him forever. (19)

Many earnest and well-meaning Christians often say, "I don't know why Jesus would die for me." Let me say, gently and kindly, that this is a works-oriented statement, not a grace-oriented statement. It fails to comprehend God's choice to create and value us so highly: He created us—all of humanity—in His image, and when we are born again, He places us in Christ. This view also fails to comprehend God's ultimate purpose in creating us—as J. I. Packer has written, "to bring into being a relationship in which He is a friend to us, and we to Him, He finding His joy in giving us gifts and we find ours in giving Him thanks" *(God Has Spoken*, 50). God sent Christ to die for us precisely because He loves us and desires eternal friendship with us. We are assured, then, of our inherent, infinite, God-given worth when we see the price God freely paid to transform rebels like us into His friends.

We must stop seeing ourselves as ducks or dogs or monkeys—or children of the world. We are children of God! We must begin seeing ourselves as God sees us and enter into His joy, His glory. Dare to accept what He is promising to give. Dare to accept the riches that are ours because we are in Christ.

CONCLUSION

If these things are true, we can make several observations:

1. Because of Christ's finished work on the cross, our deliverance from the powers of evil has already been accomplished (Ephesians 1:15–23).

2. Repentance and obedience is the key to living within the victory over the forces of darkness that Christ has already made available to us (Ephesians 2:1–10).

3. We should no longer perceive ourselves as evil or bad. Sometimes we do bad things, but we are not bad people (Ephesians 4:24).

4. We are eternally alive and eternally secure (Ephesians 1:13–14).

5. We have been transferred out of the kingdom of darkness into the kingdom of light (Colossians 1:13–14).

6. We share in Christ's divine nature (2 Peter 1:4).

7. We can have victory over sin and the powers of darkness (Romans 6:1—11).

8. We can win the battle for our mind (Romans 12:1–2; 2 Corinthians 10:3–5).

9. Christ has been given all authority in heaven and earth. We are in Christ. Therefore, Christ's authority is exercised in our behalf (Matthew 28:18; Ephesians 6:12–13).

10. I am a new creation. Old things have passed away. All things have become new! (2 Corinthians 5:17).

If we are to be victorious in the spiritual battle, one of the key ingredients is seeing ourselves as God sees us. We all tend to act consistent with how we see ourselves. That is why children who grow up in nurturing homes tend to succeed more commonly than children brought up in neglectful, affection-starved, or abusive homes. If we feel inadequate, inferior, and insecure, we tend to act accordingly, interfering with relationships and achievements. If we feel adequate, accepted, and secure, we tend to act accordingly, contributing positively to relationships and achievements.

That is why it is so important to see ourselves as God sees us. If we see ourselves as God's children, of inherent and infinite God-given worth, loved without measure and without end, headed to an eternity of glory, faith, hope, love, peace, and joy, we tend to act accordingly.

SPEED BUMP!

Slow down to be sure you've gotten the main points of this chapter.

Q1. How does God see us?

A1. God sees us *in Christ*, having been born again in righteousness and true holiness in spirit, awaiting our complete adoption, the redemption of our bodies.

Q2. What should our response be to our new identity in Christ?

A2. Our response should be *gratitude* and obedience.

FILL IN THE BLANK

Q1. How does God see us?

A1. God sees us _____, having been born again in righteousness and true holiness in spirit, awaiting our complete adoption, the redemption of our bodies.

Q2. What should our response be to our new identity in Christ?

A2. Our response should be _____ and obedience.

FOR FURTHER THOUGHT AND DISCUSSION

1. Before reading this chapter, how did you see yourself? What negative imprinting had you experienced?

2. After learning how God sees us, how do you see yourself now?

3. What would you say to a person who says, "I don't know why Jesus would die for me"?

WHAT IF I DON'T BELIEVE?

1. If I don't believe my new identity in Christ, I must ignore or disbelieve large portions of Scripture that describe me as a new creation.

2. I will tend to live like who I see myself, which will militate against success in my relations and achievements both temporal and eternal.

3. I will have limited impact on others who may be struggling with the same issues I am.

FOR FURTHER STUDY

1. Scripture

Several Scripture passages speak of the importance of our new identity in Christ:

- Romans 6–7
- 2 Corinthians 5:17
- Ephesians 1:1–14
- Ephesians 4:24

Read these passages and consider how they add to your understanding of the importance of righteousness.

2. Books

Several other books are very helpful in studying this subject further.
Victory over the Darkness, Neil Anderson
His Image, My Image, Josh McDowell
Authentic Christianity, Ray Stedman
Lifetime Guarantee, Bill Gillham

11

HOW CAN WE GAIN A CLEAR CONSCIENCE AND PULL DOWN SPIRITUAL STRONGHOLDS?

Paul Tournier, the Christian psychiatrist, used to tell a story about himself and a friend of his, a Catholic priest. Tournier said that this friend was one of the most naturally well-adjusted individuals he had ever met. He grew up in a godly home, never rebelled as a youth, and served the Lord as a priest with sincere dedication, sacrifice, and consistent joy. Tournier, in contrast with his friend, fought inner battles of faith all his life. Tournier observed that his friend served the Lord out of his considerable strength, while Tournier served the Lord out of his considerable weakness.

Tournier's comment ministered deeply to me, because his anecdote pointed to the relationship I have with a close friend of mine who is also a pastor. He grew up in a godly home, never rebelled as a youth, and regularly exhibits the fruit of the Spirit in his life and significant ministry. He is quiet, easygoing, and steadfast, serving the Lord out of his considerable strength, while I, like Tournier, serve the Lord out of my considerable weakness.

One of my considerable weaknesses exhibited itself in a humiliating and very painful way when I was in seminary. My second year, I had cheated on the final exam of a Hebrew class. There were extenuating circumstances, of course (aren't there always?). Because I got overcommitted to doing a good thing, I had gotten behind in my studies near the end of the semester. I rationalized that the Lord knew I was behind because I had to help someone out of a jam. Without passing the Hebrew final exam, I couldn't pass the course, because passing it was a course requirement, no matter how good my grades had been up to that point. If I didn't pass the course, I would have to repeat it (since it was a course required for graduation), which would require me to stay around seminary another whole year. That was unthinkable. So I cheated. I just glanced from time to time at the paper of a good student sitting next to me. I cheated only enough to pass, not enough to get an A, though I could have. The *world* would excuse me. I excused *myself*. But *God* didn't excuse me.

Sometime later, I attended a seminar in which the teacher stressed the need to have a clear conscience in order to have moral authority. "If your conscience convicts you of your own sins," the teacher said, "you will never have the moral authority to help others live holy lives." It made sense. I began to sweat. The exam loomed like a freight train coming at me from the other end of a tunnel. *Why did I ever come to this dumb seminar, anyway?* Conviction crushed me with its weight. There was no relief. As David said in the Psalms, "My vitality was drained away as with the fever heat of summer" (32:4 NASB).

The teacher said we needed to make a list of all the people the Lord brought to our mind whom we needed to forgive and others from whom we needed to seek forgiveness. My Hebrew professor headed my list. It was unthinkable that I go back and confess that sin to him. What would he think of me? What would he do to me? I might get kicked out of school!

Over the days that followed, the pain of the conviction grew so great that it was easier to envision confessing the sin to my professor and taking whatever consequence he dealt me than it was to continue living under the conviction. My misery too great to bear, I went to my professor, confessed my sin, and asked if he would forgive me. He was very gracious, forgave me, and levied on me a very fair consequence.

IN THIS CHAPTER WE LEARN THAT . . .

1. A clear conscience is one free of guilt, not because we've never sinned, but because we've responded biblically to our sin.

2. We can gain a clear conscience by repenting of known sin, forgiving those who've wronged us, and seeking forgiveness from those we have wronged.

3. We can protect our conscience from evil influences by repenting from and renouncing anything we may be doing or may have done in the past that has made us vulnerable to demonic influence.

I walked out of his office with a feeling of freedom and joy that is difficult to describe. I had rarely known such wonderful freedom.

It would have been great if that had been the only sin I had to confess, but during the seminar, the Lord brought to my mind a whole page full of people I had to forgive or seek forgiveness from. It was one of the hardest experiences of my life, but by the time I crossed off the last name on the list, I had a freedom that I had never known. I have maintained this freedom (though not perfectly), because whenever the Lord has brought to mind a sin I needed to deal with, either forgiving or seeking forgiveness, I have always followed through. So I can preach, teach, and share my faith with conviction because my conscience does not accuse me. I shudder to think of the moral junkyard that would be rusting and rotting at the bottom of my heart if I had not learned this critical truth early in my Christian experience.

WHAT IS A CLEAR CONSCIENCE?

A clear conscience is one free of guilt, not because we've never
sinned, but because we've responded biblically to our sin.

One time I heard the true story of a lady who was restoring the gilt of a lovely, antique gold-leaf picture frame. She needed some additional repair materials so she went to a hardware store and asked the clerk, "Do you have any gilt?" The clerk replied, "Sometimes it's almost unbearable." Well, first we laugh, and then we cry. It's funny because the clerk misunderstood and was so readily transparent about her inner struggles. It's sad because so many people walk around with a truckload of guilt on their shoulders.

I have come to believe that a clear conscience is essential not only to moral authority in our personal ministry, but also to victory in spiritual warfare. A number of Scripture passages, when taken together, show us that if we allow ourselves to go through life without keeping our conscience clear, the devil can shipwreck our lives:

1. The apostle Paul considered a clear conscience a top priority in his own personal life:

   I have lived my life with a perfectly good conscience before God up to this day (Acts 23:1 NASB).

   and,

   I also do my best to maintain always a blameless conscience both before God and before men (Acts 24:16 NASB).

2. The Scriptures teach that one goal of biblical instruction is a good conscience. We see from this passage that a good conscience is linked to a pure heart:

But the goal of our instruction is love from a pure heart and a good conscience and a sincere faith (1 Timothy 1:5 NASB).

3. The Scriptures give us examples of people who rejected the importance of keeping a good conscience, and in doing so, brought shipwreck to their lives:

. . . keeping faith and a *good conscience,* which some *have rejected and suffered shipwreck in regard to their faith.* Among these are Hymenaeus and Alexander, whom I have handed over to Satan, so that they will be taught not to blaspheme (1 Timothy 1:19–20 NASB, emphasis added).

4. The apostle James teaches us that if we have bitterness, jealousy, and selfish ambition in our hearts (which would prohibit having a clear conscience), our best wisdom would be earthly, natural, and demonic:

Who among you is wise and understanding? Let him show by his good behavior his deeds in the gentleness of wisdom. But if you have bitter jealousy and selfish ambition in your heart, do not be arrogant and so lie against the truth. This wisdom is not that which comes down from above, but is earthly, natural, demonic (James 3:13–15 NASB).

5. The apostle Paul furthers this line of thought by teaching us that when anyone does not repent (one cannot have a clear conscience if he is knowingly unrepentant) of known sin, they can be ensnared by the devil, being held captive to do his will:

And the Lord's bondservant must not be quarrelsome, but be kind to all, able to teach, patient when wronged, with gentleness *correcting those who are in opposition,* if perhaps God may grant them *repentance* leading to the knowledge of the truth, and they may come to their senses and *escape from the snare of the devil,* having been held captive by him to do his will (2 Timothy 2:24–26 NASB, emphasis added).

These passages plainly indicate that a clear conscience is essential to the Christian life and victory in spiritual warfare.

HOW CAN WE GAIN A CLEAR CONSCIENCE?

We can gain a clear conscience by repenting of known sin, forgiving those who've wronged us, and seeking forgiveness from those we have wronged.

The Bible instructs us to forgive those who've wronged us (Ephesians 4:32) and not to harbor bitterness (Hebrews 12:15). The Holy Spirit convicts one of sin, including the sin of unforgiveness. If we go to the Lord in prayer to tell Him we are willing to do whatever is necessary to gain a clear conscience, and then ask the Holy Spirit to reveal to us anyone we have not forgiven for wronging us, the Holy Spirit will show us those people. We may need to make a list of them. Then we ask the Lord to give us the grace to forgive whoever comes to mind. Finally, in an act of our will, we tell the Lord that, by His grace, we forgive that person for wronging us. In some cases, it might be helpful to tell the person we have forgiven them, especially if there has been a breach in the relationship. In other cases, the person may not even be aware of our feelings, or might not even be alive. However the Lord leads us in that decision, we have gained a conscience clear of unforgiveness.

> ### WHY I NEED TO KNOW THIS
>
> One of the keys to victory in the spiritual war is repenting of known sin and keeping one's conscience free. If I don't know this, I may violate the principle and live in perpetual defeat.

But in gaining a clear conscience, the need for forgiveness has a flip side: we also need to ask the Lord to reveal to us anyone whom we have wronged and have not asked for forgiveness. Sometimes when the Holy Spirit reveals our sin to us, it may be a wrong action (or attitude) that we have committed privately, not something that we've done directly against another person or that affected another person directly. In these cases our confession and repentance need only go to the Lord. But when the Holy Spirit reveals that we have wronged someone else, we must seek their forgiveness as well. We commit to make restitution if it is appropriate (sometimes it is not—we must follow the Lord's leading). Then, we begin contacting the people, asking them to forgive us for wronging them. There are several crucial steps in the process of seeking forgiveness, many of which are observed in the repentant prodigal son (Luke 15:11–32):

1. We should pray that the Lord will prepare their heart to accept our repentance and forgive us.

2. We should talk to the person directly, either face-to-face or over the phone. Written communication can be imprecise, time-consuming, and incriminating for someone to use improperly.

3. We should not rehash the details, but should identify the basic offense. For example, you may have gotten angry and shouted insults at someone. The basic offense was of letting your anger get the better of you and treating the other person with disrespect and unkindness. There is no need to repeat the insulting words when confessing your wrong behavior; rather you might identify your offense by saying something like, "The Lord has shown me how wrong I was when I shouted at you and treated you with such disrespect. I can see how that must have hurt you, and I would like you to please forgive me." It is important to ask for forgiveness with sincerity. If the other person doubts your true repentance, it may only make things worse.

4. We should be prepared for their response:

The person may say, "No." However, at this point, you have discharged your responsibility to confess your wrong and seek forgiveness, and the matter is now on his shoulders. If given the opportunity you could acknowledge your disappointment and your hope that he might be willing to forgive you in the future. Then you can continue to pray that the Lord will work in his heart and will direct you if He wants you to try again at a later time.

The person may say, "Oh, don't worry about it. It wasn't so bad." In that case, ask again so that you can both have closure on the issue of forgiveness. Say something like, "I appreciate your understanding. Does that mean you are willing to forgive me?" Or, "I appreciate your understanding. I am so sorry for hurting you the way I did. It would mean a great deal to me to know that you forgive me." Use your own judgment in knowing how far to press this, but since this person is obviously willing, it's important that you both walk away from the conversation feeling that wrong has been repented of and forgiveness has been asked for and given.

The person may say, "Yes, I forgive you." In that case we should not allow the memory of our wrongdoing to continue to plague us, but enjoy the restored fellowship and a conscience free of guilt.

If we find, however, that we are being plagued and wearied from constantly dealing with negative thoughts or temptations to the same sin, we may be doing battle against a spiritual stronghold.

HOW CAN WE PROTECT OUR CONSCIENCE FROM EVIL INFLUENCES AND PULL DOWN SPIRITUAL STRONGHOLDS?

We can protect our conscience from evil influences by
repenting from and renouncing anything we may be doing or may have
done in the past that has made us vulnerable to demonic influence.

A common strategic maneuver in military warfare is that of establishing a stronghold, and it is a common strategy of our enemy in spiritual warfare as well. Consider 2 Corinthians 10:3–6:

> For though we walk in the flesh, we do not war according to the flesh. For the weapons of our warfare are not carnal but mighty in God for pulling down strongholds, casting down arguments and every high thing that exalts itself against the knowledge of God, bringing every thought into captivity to the obedience of Christ, and being ready to punish all disobedience when your obedience is fulfilled.

A stronghold is a place where a concentration of power exists that is difficult or impossible to overthrow. In the 1800s, the Badlands of South Dakota were said to be a stronghold for gunmen and outlaws. It was their territory, and no lawman dared intrude. The Northeast is still said to be a stronghold of political liberalism. Italy and Sicily are said to be strongholds of Mafia activity.

If there is a stronghold in a Christian's life, it is a concentration of power difficult for the Christian to overcome. The strongholds in the context of this passage are attitudes about God that were unbiblical ("arguments and every high thing that exalts itself against the knowledge of God"), and disobedience to the truth. These unbiblical attitudes and acts of disobedience were a stronghold in the Corinthian church brought on by the teachings of false apostles, ministers of Satan (2 Corinthians 11:13–15). Any wrong line of thinking or any area of habitual disobedience can develop into a stronghold.

> **Our unbiblical attitudes can be one of Satan's strongholds.**

The apostle Paul says that these strongholds are not brought down by human ability. The metaphor here probably depicts literal weapons of war such as: swords, spears, bows and arrows, battering rams, and catapults for throwing balls of fire onto an opponent. The more figurative weapons of war might include intellectual cleverness, money, persuasive speech, political influence, clever strategies, and so on.

Such weapons are not effective in destroying spiritual strongholds in a person's life. Rather, the weapons of faith, prayer, the Scripture, repentance, obedience, spiritual wisdom, and standing firm destroy spiritual strongholds.

Areas of struggle in the spiritual warfare that might indicate a spiritual stronghold at work are:

- Demonic harassment—possible manifestations might include feelings of oppression, sudden and chilling fear, nightmares, demonic apparitions, hearing voices (sometimes encouraging suicide or murder), physical heaviness on the chest, difficulty breathing, etc.
- Addictions—such as food, alcohol, drugs, tobacco, television, sex, lying, procrastination, materialism, pornography, rock music, or any number of other sins that have taken up residence in your life and have become so strong that you find it almost impossible to overcome.
- Emotional bondages—such as an attitude of intellectual superiority that prompts you to sit in judgment over the Bible, deciding which passages you will believe and which ones you won't. Pride is the mother hen under which all other sins are hatched, said C. S. Lewis. It is a common emotional stronghold, as are worry, fear, anger, a spirit of independence and rebellion against authority, sarcasm, unkindness, a loose tongue, bitterness, resentment, jealousy, a lack of forgiveness, depression, suicidal thoughts, etc.

If we are being demonically harassed, or finding it impossible to overcome an addiction or negative emotion, we need to consider the possibility of a spiritual stronghold. The stronghold might have developed from *past* as well as *present* involvement in unbiblical beliefs or activities that we've never repudiated or repented of, and have therefore made us vulnerable to demonic influences. We therefore need to examine our beliefs and behaviors in light of scriptural truth and principles, "bringing every thought (and activity) into captivity to the obedience of Christ."

Negative emotions can be Satan's strongholds.

Three areas of our life need to be examined: occult and related activities, cults and other false religions, and ancestral demonic connections.

Occult and Related Activities. It seems that several types of present and past activities tend to make some people vulnerable to demonic influence in their lives. Any activity that is energized by demons, for example, may open a door of influence for demons into some people's lives. These could include things like playing with a Ouija board; attending a seance; seeing a fortune-teller; playing with tarot cards;

paying attention to astrology; playing role-playing games like Dungeons & Dragons; playing some occult-type computer games; attempting paranormal activity such as astral projection, clairvoyance, or any kind of magic; being interested in or participating in witchcraft, the occult, animal sacrifice, or ritual sexual involvement; reading or looking at pornography; reading or watching horror stories, and so on. The list here is not complete, but anything that you suspect could possibly have demonic influence belongs on the list. While the Bible does not specifically mention all of these activities by name, we have the biblical mandate in Deuteronomy 18:9–13 to not be involved in any way with anything that is demonic.

Therefore, when trying to gain a clear conscience from evil influences, these things need to be considered and renounced. To clear your conscience from any past or present suspect activities, ask the Lord to reveal to you any involvement you might have had or currently have in any activities that could have made you vulnerable to demonic influences.

1. Review the spiritual armor, and make sure you do not have any holes in your personal righteousness.

2. Discontinue any present involvement in any of these or other suspect activities.

3. If you have participated in any of these things in the past, renounce them and your participation in them, and get rid of anything you have that is associated with them (such as a Ouija board, tarot cards, etc.).

4. Voice your repentance to the Lord, commit to Him your ongoing repudiation of these activities.

5. Ask the Lord to break any influence these things might have in your life.

6. Ask the Lord to protect you from any deception or harm and to keep you secure, as you stand firm in your position in Christ, who has already won the victory for you.

After reviewing this process, you might pray as follows:

Dear Father in heaven,
I acknowledge that I have participated in (whatever the Lord brings to your mind in this area), and confess it as sin. I repudiate (whatever it is), ask Your forgiveness, and accept Your offer of full restoration of fellowship. I pray You will break any demonic influence this involvement may have in my life, and keep me safe, as I stand firm in Christ. In His name, Amen.

Cults and Other False Religions. In addition to these occult-type activities, an involvement or interest of any kind in cult activity also seems to open a door to demonic influence in some people's lives. The New Age Movement, Masons, Scientology, the Unification Church, and others must be suspect. Other false religions such as Buddhism, Hare Krishna, Hinduism, Transcendental Meditation, Yoga, and Islam might also play a similar role (1 Timothy 4:1).

> Certain beliefs can make a person vulnerable to demonic activity.

Many people who have engaged in one or more of these activities have experienced no known demonic repercussions. On the other hand, others have apparently experienced serious demonic repercussions from only one of these things. Therefore, when trying to gain a clear conscience from evil influences, these things need to be considered and renounced. To clear your conscience from any past or present suspect activities, ask the Lord to reveal to you any involvement you might have had or currently have in any activities that could have made you vulnerable to demonic activity:

1. Review the spiritual armor, and make sure you do not have any holes in your personal righteousness.

2. Discontinue any present involvement in any of these or other suspect activities.

3. If you have participated in any of these things in the past, renounce them and your participation in them, and get rid of anything you have that is associated with them (such as religious statues and symbols).

4. Voice your repentance to the Lord, commit to Him your ongoing repudiation of these activities.

5. Ask the Lord to break any influence these things might have in your life.

6. Ask the Lord to protect you from any deception or harm and to keep you secure, as you stand firm in your position in Christ, who has already won the victory for you.

After reviewing this process, you might pray as follows:

Dear Father in heaven,
I acknowledge that I have participated in (whatever the Lord brings to your mind in this area), and confess it as sin. I repudiate (whatever it is), ask Your forgiveness, and accept Your offer of full restoration of fellowship. I pray You will break any demonic influence

this involvement may have in my life, and keep me safe, as I stand firm in Christ. In His name, Amen.

Ancestral Demonic Connections. There is one last area of potential stronghold that is somewhat controversial. Some ministers and counselors who are experienced in spiritual warfare issues believe that they see a genealogical link to demonic vulnerability. That is, if ancestors have been involved in demonic activities (the occult, psychic involvement, etc.), descendants are vulnerable to demonic influence. They will often quote Exodus 20:4–5:

> You shall not make for yourself a carved image—any likeness of anything that is in heaven above, or that is in the earth beneath, or that is in the water under the earth; you shall not bow down to them nor serve them. For I, the LORD your God, am a jealous God, visiting the iniquity of the fathers upon the children to the third and fourth generations of those who hate Me.

Therefore, these counselors teach, you must renounce the sins of your ancestors and any curses that may have been placed on you.

Others, however, take strong exception to this teaching. Though the Old Testament does clearly say that God visits the sins of the fathers on the children to the third and fourth generations, He does so only on "those who hate Me." Exodus 20:6, however, states, "but showing mercy to thousands, to those who love Me and keep my commandments." In Deuteronomy 7:9 we read,

> Therefore know that the LORD your God, He is God, the faithful God who keeps covenant and mercy for a thousand generations with those who love Him and keep His commandments.

And further, in Ezekiel 18:20, we read,

> The soul who sins shall die. The son shall not bear the guilt of the father, nor the father bear the guilt of the son. The righteousness of the righteous shall be upon himself, and the wickedness of the wicked shall be upon himself.

The weight of these passages suggest, say other counselors and teachers, that when a descendant of someone who was involved in demonic activities (knowingly or unknowingly) becomes a Christian, it breaks the cycle of sin being visited on the heads of children, and starts a new upward cycle of righteousness, unless someone new breaks that cycle.

Perhaps the answer is that a prayer of ancestral renunciation might be helpful at some times, just to demonstrate to the demonic world that the person praying is not going to follow the path of his or her ancestors. The same thing might be accomplished by spiritual growth, righteous living, and resisting the devil in all areas of life. My own opinion, and it is only an opinion, is that a prayer of ancestral repudiation is not essential to living free of demonic involvement, and is especially not needed if the person shows no signs of demonic influence. But if a person with a family history of demonic involvement also shows signs of demonic susceptibility or vulnerability, a prayer of family renunciation might be a good way of making it clear to everyone—humans and demons alike—that the cycle is broken!

If someone considers that a prayer of ancestral renunciation is necessary, he might pray something like:

Dear Heavenly Father,

I come to You as one who has been forgiven, redeemed and born again, transferred out of the kingdom of darkness into the kingdom of Your beloved Son. I renounce any involvement in demonic activity which my ancestors have had, and reject any possible claim which Satan may feel he has on me because of my family. I claim the truth of Your Word, that You show mercy to thousands, to those who love You and keep Your commandments, and that the son shall not bear the guilt of the father, nor the father bear the guilt of the son. The righteousness of the righteous shall be upon himself. I now claim the biblical promise that the cycle is broken, and I commit myself to You as an instrument of righteousness, to glorify You in my body. I pray in the name of Jesus, who has made my freedom possible. Amen.

CONCLUSION

It is the truth, not spiritual technique, that will set you free (John 8:32). In Matthew 4, Jesus was tempted by Satan three times, and each time Jesus answered the temptation with Scripture. If Jesus needed to rely on Scripture to defeat the devil, how much more do we!

You may experience freedom after going through these prayers, only to feel later that you are under spiritual attack again. This would not be surprising. In Luke 4, Jesus triumphs over Satan's tempting Him in the wilderness, but, the Scripture continues, "when the devil had ended every temptation, he departed from Him until an opportune time" (v. 13). When you are victorious over spiritual attack, do not be surprised if it recurs at what the demons consider to be an opportune time. It follows, then, that consistent faithfulness to the Lord is important, because when you dabble in sin or jump off the deep end, you will be especially vulnerable to demonic deception.

Pastor and Bible teacher J. Vernon McGee once said that someone told him if "his time had not come" he could walk out in rush-hour traffic on the freeway in Los Angeles and not get hurt. McGee replied, "My friend, that may be true, but if you walk out in rush-hour traffic on the freeway in Los Angeles, I'm here to tell you, your time *has* come."

In the same way, if you decide to wade around in sin, or jump off the deep end, it *is* a "more opportune time" for the devil.

SPEED BUMP!

Slow down to be sure you have gotten the main points of this chapter.

Q1. What is a clear conscience?

A1. A clear conscience is one free of guilt, not because we've never sinned, but because we've responded *biblically* to our sin.

Q2. How can we gain a clear conscience ?

A2. We can gain a clear conscience by *repenting* of known sin, forgiving those who've wronged us, and seeking forgiveness from those we have wronged.

Q3. How can we protect our conscience from evil influences and pull down spiritual strongholds?

A3. We can protect our conscience from evil influences by repenting from and *renouncing* anything we may be doing or may have done in the past that has made us vulnerable to demonic influence.

FILL IN THE BLANK

Q1 What is a clear conscience?

A1. A clear conscience is one free of guilt, not because we've never sinned, but because we've responded _____ to our sin.

Q2. How can we gain a clear conscience?

A2. We can gain a clear conscience by _____ of known sin, forgiving those who've wronged us, and seeking forgiveness from those we have wronged.

Q3. How can we protect our conscience from evil influences and pull down spiritual strongholds?

A3. We can protect our conscience from evil influences by repenting from and _____ anything we may be doing or may have done in the past that has made us vulnerable to demonic influence.

FOR FURTHER THOUGHT AND DISCUSSION

1. Do you feel unresolved guilt over things you have done in the past? What do you think you need to do to resolve the guilt?

2. Have you ever engaged in any activities that you think may have made you vulnerable to demonic influence? If you have, how do you think you should respond?

3. Are you aware of any demonic involvement on the part of anyone in your family, past or present? Do you think you need to pray a prayer of ancestral renunciation?

WHAT IF I DON'T BELIEVE?

1. I risk allowing my heart to become a rusting junkyard of unresolved sin.

2. I risk giving demons a foothold in my life because of moral failure.

3. I risk giving demons a foothold in my life because of present or past inappropriate activities.

FOR FURTHER STUDY

1. Scripture

- John 8:44
- Ephesians 6:10–18
- James 4:7
- 1 Peter 5:8

2. Books

Several other books are very helpful in studying this subject. They are listed below according to the view they support. Read them all with care and discernment. There may be things in all of them that you don't agree with. Just because you read something in one of the books that you do not agree with does not mean it is all bad. I have read all these books and found each of them helpful in coming to my own convictions regarding spiritual warfare.

The Bondage Breaker, Neil Anderson

Lifetime Guarantee, Bill Gillham

The Lies We Believe, Chris Thurman

3. Resources

"Healing through the Destruction of Strongholds" by Kay Arthur, a taped message available on video or audio from:

Precept Ministries
P.O. Box 182218
Chattanooga, TN 37422-7218
800-763-8280

12

HOW CAN WE STAND FIRM IN THE WAR?

Without courage, all other virtues lose their meaning.
—**Winston Churchill**

When I was in the third grade, our class had a bully. I don't remember how I did it, but I crossed him one day, and he put the word out that he was going to beat me up. For a number of weeks, terror ruled my life. I looked around every corner before turning it. I found out where he was on the playground and made sure he never saw me. Ronnie (not his real name) dominated my life.

But fear can wear on a fellow. I got very weary of the fear, of always looking over my shoulder, and of making excuses why I couldn't play a certain game (because Ronnie was there). He was coming in from the playground one day when I was going out, and we crossed in the hallway. Following his normal procedure, he stalked over to me and asked me if I wanted to fight. Something deep down inside me snapped. I faced him squarely and said, "Yes!" There was a "throw-yourself-in-front-of-the-train" look in my eye, I suspect, the look of someone who has been through so much that he no longer cares what happens to him. I wasn't only ready to fight the bully; I was ready to fight the increasingly unbearable weight of fear and had decided that a third-grade terrorist couldn't do anything to me worse than what the fear was doing. I was in a philosophical war, and my harasser was simply the focal point, the precipitant. Well, the look on my face must have unnerved my tormentor, for he seemed to turn to JELL-O. This tough guy who stood six inches taller than I and who outweighed me by ten or fifteen pounds (which is significant when you weigh only eighty pounds to begin with) suddenly couldn't fight. He rushed off to class.

I was never bothered by him again.

This is what we must do to the forces of darkness. We must turn and face them and be ready to do battle with them.

139

IN THIS CHAPTER WE LEARN THAT . . .

1. Christians can be influenced by demons, so we must always be on guard spiritually.

2. We can be protected from the forces of darkness by a life of obedience to the Scripture and of trusting God to protect us.

3. Believers are not all agreed on whether or not exorcisms are valid, but do agree that lasting liberty for demonized persons depends on their cooperation.

4. We can help others in the spiritual war by taking them through a process of cleansing their conscience and using prayer and Scripture to resist demonic influence.

However, we must be clear on one very important difference between fighting a person and fighting the forces of darkness. If it had come to it, I would have fought the class bully in my own strength (and probably lost). But we cannot fight the forces of darkness in our own strength. We must do battle God's way and in His power.

CAN CHRISTIANS BE INFLUENCED BY DEMONS?

Christians can be influenced by demons, so we must always be on guard spiritually.

Christians need not fear demonic influence if they are following the biblical instructions on how to live above demonic oppression (be alert, put on the armor, and resist). If the Christian gives himself over to sin, however, he has much to fear!

We see in 1 Corinthians 5:1–5 that a Christian in the church in Corinth was living in dreadful immorality. The result was satanic exposure as judgment on his sin.

> It is actually reported that there is immorality among you, and immorality of such a kind as does not exist even among the Gentiles, that someone has his father's wife. You have become arrogant and have not mourned instead, so that the one who had done this deed would be removed from your midst. For I, on my part, though absent in body but present in spirit, have already judged him who has so committed this, as though I were present. In the name of our Lord Jesus, when you are assembled, and I with you in spirit, with the power of our Lord Jesus, I have decided to deliver such a one to Satan for the destruction of his flesh, so that his spirit may be saved in the day of the Lord Jesus. (NASB)

What a powerful and dramatic judgment, for a Christian to fall into the hands of Satan. However, as the apostle Paul points out, the "destruction of his flesh" is a temporal judgment that the Christian suffers so that he might not lose his eternal soul. This destruction probably included the cause-effect consequences of a life given over to sin. In addition, however, this punishment could possibly involve demonization. It should be a stark warning to any child of God who feels free to live like the devil.

HOW CAN WE BE PROTECTED FROM THE FORCES OF DARKNESS?

*We can be protected from the forces of darkness by a life of obedience
to the Scripture and of trusting God to protect us.*

Ephesians 6:10 says, "Finally, my brethren, be strong in the Lord and in the power of His might." That makes it clear that we are not to battle the forces of darkness in our own strength. A teaching going around today leads one to believe that because we have been raised up with Christ and seated with Him and because He has authority over all other principalities and powers, we also have authority over all other principalities and powers. We must be very cautious about how we understand this truth. Our strength is in the Lord. We have no strength in and of ourselves to be victorious in battles against demons.

After the apostle Paul instructs us to be strong in the Lord and in the power of His might, he then goes on to say, "Put on the whole armor of God, that you may be able to stand against the wiles of the devil" (v. 11). The armor, of course, typifies Jesus, His righteousness, and His truth. If we were to try to battle demonic forces in our own strength, we would face the spiritual equivalent of a paper shredder—with our being the paper. Demons are so much more intelligent and powerful than we that we have only one avenue of safety: Jesus. We stand in Him, and in His armor. Then and only then can we stand firm.

The greatest weapons demons have are ignorance and fear. Once we learn that their power over us is limited to our *allowing* them to have power over us; and once we take the steps Scripture tells us to take to be free from their influence, we need not fear demons. Their power over us is limited.

Specifically, to "stand firm" means that we reject their suggestions, temptations, and insinuations. We deny them their scare tactics. We claim our security and freedom in Christ, and we quote appropriate Scripture passages to them, as Jesus did in His temptation in Matthew 4.

There is a very helpful progression of passages that we can quote as our personal affirmations whenever we suspect that we are under spiritual attack:

1. *Alert!* First, we must be alert for the potential of spiritual attack: I am of sober spirit and alert to Satan's tactics. I know that my adversary, the devil, prowls about like a roaring lion, seeking someone to devour.

2. *Armor!* Second, we must affirm that we have the armor in place in our lives:

   Belt of Truth: I accept the truth of the Bible and choose to follow it with integrity.

   Breastplate of Righteousness: I will not harbor known sin, and I will strive to live like Christ.

   Shoes of the Gospel of Peace: I believe the promises of God and count on them to be true for me.

   Shield of Faith: Whenever I feel like doubting or sinning or quitting, I will reject those thoughts and feelings and declare to myself the truth.

   Helmet of Salvation: I rest my hope in the future and live in this world according to the value system of the next.

   Sword of the Spirit: I will use the Scriptures specifically in life's situations to fend off attacks of the Enemy and put him to flight.

3. *Resist!* Third, we must claim the truth of Scripture and call upon the forces of darkness to obey the Scriptures and flee from us:

   I am in Christ, and I am a new creation (2 Corinthians 5:17).

   The blood of Jesus Christ, [God's] Son cleanses me from all sin (1 John 1:7).

   Greater is He who is in me than he who is in the world (1 John 4:4).

   I submit to God. I resist the devil and his forces of darkness. According to the authority of Jesus and the Word of God, I declare that he must flee from me (James 4:7).

I remain in an attitude of prayer as I continually ask God to strengthen me, guide me, and keep me safe. Note that this collection of affirmations from Scripture is neither a formula nor an incantation. It is not elaborate hocus-pocus, nor a verbal "silver cross" that automatically drives away evil. It is not a clever technique that can be taught even to those choosing to live in sin. All this process can do is help a sincere person review the key elements in spiritual warfare. But if the words do not reflect a person's heart attitude, nothing in Scripture suggests that it will "work like magic."

SHOULD CHRISTIANS
CAST DEMONS OUT OF OTHERS?

Believers are not all agreed on whether or not exorcisms are valid, but they do agree
that lasting liberty for demonized persons depends on their cooperation.

At this point in the book it should come as no surprise to learn that believers are divided as to whether or not Christians should cast demons out of others (that is, practice exorcism). Some believe that it is a valid ministry when called for, and others discourage it. Again, it is necessary to generalize in order not to get buried by details. Generally speaking, those who believe that exorcism is valid today (or the broader notions of "power encounters" and "deliverance ministries") see it as rather straightforward, uncomplicated, and easy to explain biblically. Jesus cast demons out of people, He commissioned His disciples to cast demons out of people (Luke 10:17–20), and that authority is reiterated by the apostle Paul in Ephesians 1:20–22 and 2:6 in which Christ's authority over demons is given to us by virtue of the fact that we are raised with Christ and seated with Him, in authority, in the heavenly places. Nowhere in the Bible is that authority rescinded. When we meet someone who is demonized, it is valid for us to help him by casting the demon out of him in the authority and name of Jesus.

Responsible "power encounter," or "deliverance," ministers urge that pre- and post-deliverance counseling be given so that when the demonized person gains freedom, he will be spiritually strengthened and prepared so that the demon(s) would not come back, possibly even in greater numbers (Matthew 12:43–45). They can point to much success following this procedure.

Those who do not believe in casting demons out of others have a more complicated perspective, one perhaps less easy to explain. As we have seen before, some view the examples of exorcisms in the Gospels and Acts as being temporary, vested primarily in Jesus and His original disciples.

There are no hard lines dividing their ministry and the ministry of future generations of Christians, but generally it is seen as a first-century phenomenon.

The later information in the Epistles to churches and pastors gives no instructions on exorcisms or dramatic demonic encounters. Rather, they focus on spiritual maturity, character, holy living, and knowledge of the truth. In Ephesians 6:11 we are told to "stand firm." In James 4:7, we are told to resist the devil. In 1 Peter 5:8–9 we are told to resist the devil and he will flee from us.

If "power encounters" exorcisms and deliverance ministries were supposed to be part of the ministry of the church, the argument goes, we would have been instructed to do it, and how to do it. The silence seems very loud.

Another question is whether or not we have authority over demons. We have already seen that the "spiritual resistance" advocates do not believe we have authority over demons. Some Christians feel free to rebuke demons and the devil. However, others do not, citing that even Michael the archangel dared not bring against Satan a reviling accusation, but said, "The Lord rebuke you" (Jude 9). And, in Zechariah 3:2, we read, "And the LORD said to Satan, 'The LORD rebuke you, Satan!'"

In addition, those who do not advocate exorcisms are concerned that, unless a demonized person is willing to put on the spiritual armor and resist the devil himself, he may not really be helped in the long run by an exorcism. In Matthew 12:43–45 we read:

> When an unclean spirit goes out of a man, he goes through dry places, seeking rest, and finds none. Then he says, "I will return to my house from which I came." And when he comes, he finds it empty, swept, and put in order. Then he goes and takes with him seven other spirits more wicked than himself, and they enter and dwell there; and the last state of that man is worse than the first.

The concern is that pre- and post-deliverance counseling is not sufficient to prepare a person for exorcism.

Unless the one who is troubled by demons is willing to put on the spiritual armor and stand firm, we may actually make his condition worse if a demon is cast out of him by someone else. If a person is really willing to turn his life over to Christ, the Epistles suggest that he can be brought to a place where he exorcises the demon himself by his own embracing of the truth and resistance to the demon(s). Certainly, this may take support and coaching from others in what might seem similar to an exorcism, but the difference is that the demonized person himself, not a third party, is responsible for the demon(s) leaving.

One popular spiritual-warfare author, Neil Anderson, wrote:

> Ultimate responsibility for spiritual freedom belongs to the individual believer, not an outside agent. It's not what you do as the counselor that counts; it's what the counselee believes, confesses, renounces, forgives, etc. You cannot take the steps to freedom for anyone but yourself. If you are successful in casting a demon out of someone without his or her involvement, what is to keep it from coming back when you leave? Unless the individual takes responsibility for his own freedom, he may end up like the poor fellow who was freed from one spirit only to be occupied by seven others who were worse than the first (Matthew 12:43–45).

> I have not attempted to "cast out a demon" in several years. But I have seen hundreds of people find freedom in Christ as I helped them resolve their personal and spiritual conflicts. I no longer deal directly with demons . . . I only work with their victims. Helping people understand the truth and assume personal responsibility for truth in their life is the essence of ministry. (*The Bondage Breaker*, 208)

On the other hand, the "power encounter" ministers have a good deal to say about these concerns. First, regarding the silence of the Epistles regarding exorcisms, they would respond that some of the Epistles were written during the same period covered in the book of Acts when exorcisms were being performed, and would call for an integration of the record in Acts with the record in the Epistles, rather than a separation of the two records.

Second, they point to church history to verify the continuation of the ministry of exorcism in the church beyond the time of the apostles. After the death of the last apostle, John, and after the New Testament writings were completed, church leaders such as Justin Martyr and Tertullian continued to report an active ministry of exorcism. Such ministry continued into the Middle Ages, but it became burdened with nonbiblical superstitious practices including literal witch-hunting. Some Protestant Reformers reacted against these abuses by abolishing the ministry of exorcism altogether. But neither the abuses nor the denial of the validity of exorcism affects the reality of demonic activity and the need for those victimized to receive full liberation in Christ. The *Evangelical Dictionary of Theology* acknowledges the validity of such a responsible ministry today and notes that "emphasis on . . . deliverance from possession through the . . . power of Jesus Christ is completely consistent with the N[ew] T[estament] and does not at all reflect the abuses or superstitions associated with the Middle Ages" (308).

Third, regarding the question in Matthew 12:43–45 suggesting that an individual must deal with sin in his life or else an exorcism may actually backfire, Ed Murphy wrote:

> Until the bondage to the flesh is broken ... effective deliverance is not possible for demonized believers. Where it does occur, it will not usually be lasting. *The expulsion of one group of evil spirits from a human life will usually lead to the entry of another group if the sin in the life to which the former demonic spirits had attached themselves is not removed.* The believer must begin to put to death the works of the flesh to become victorious in the sin war which involves him. If not, he will soon become a war casualty. (*The Handbook for Spiritual Warfare*, 109)

Regarding whether or not a believer can fall into such terrible sin that he becomes demonized to the point of physical inhabitation by a demon, the power encounter ministers would point to the Christian in 1 Corinthians 5:1–5. He was committing fornication with his stepmother, a sin that everyone will admit is reprehensible. Paul said that he had decided that the church should "deliver such a one to Satan for the destruction of the flesh, that his spirit may be saved in the day of the Lord Jesus" (v. 5). It seems very possible that being "delivered over to Satan for the destruction of his flesh" could easily (maybe probably) involve demonization even to the point of inhabitation. This passage seems to say that Christians can fall into dreadful sin, and that that sin can lead to being given over to Satan.

Finally, regarding the need for the victim of demonization to exert his will in order for the exorcism to have a lasting effect, Ed Murphy again wrote that when he casts out a demon, he does so only after binding the demon(s) to keep it from controlling the person's mind:

> The demons are shut down. They are forbidden to manifest themselves and even to hinder the thinking process of the unsaved person. It is our authority in Christ which brings them under control. With some, admittedly, this may not work or works with great difficulty. The immediate goal is always the same, both with the unbelievers and believers, however. It is, wherever possible, to have the counselee fully lucid and in control of his mind while we minister to him. (See Neil Anderson's excellent outline of this procedure in *Released from Bondage* . . . 183–247). Thus the power encounter becomes a "truth encounter," a term I learned from Neil Anderson. Even power encounters are really truth encounters as it is the truth of God's power working through our life (and, in the case of the demonized believers, through their life also) that we rely upon to bring demonic powers into submission. (561)

On this final point, then, the three primary views concerning spiritual warfare differ very little: whatever may be done by others for persons troubled by demons (and here the views do disagree), each view insists that full and lasting liberty in Christ depends on the counselee's cooperation with the Word and Spirit of God in confessing sin, renouncing demonic attachments, and walking in holiness.

HOW CAN WE HELP OTHERS IN THE SPIRITUAL WAR?

We can help others in the spiritual war by taking them through a process of cleansing their conscience and using prayer and Scripture to resist demonic influence.

As I have said, I prefer to exercise great caution when helping others struggling with personal problems that might stem from demonic influence. It has been my observation that counselors tend to fall into one of two camps, and there is very little crossover between the camps. The two camps are the "psychological" model and the "spiritual warfare" model.

The psychological-model counselors tend to put very little credence in demonic influence as the cause of emotional problems. The spiritual-warfare–model counselors tend to rely very heavily on getting rid of demonic influence as the primary avenue for improvement. Because I am not a trained counselor, I have some capacity to stand back, observe, and try to understand why both sides can point to success and failures.

In fact, I asked a psychological-model counselor who had had some exposure to spiritual-warfare counseling why he didn't use the spiritual-warfare approaches in his counseling. He replied that in his practice he saw what he considered to be "too many" people who had been through spiritual-warfare counseling, and it hadn't worked. They were desperate for help, which he felt he gave them.

> ## WHY I NEED TO KNOW THIS
>
> I need to know this so that I will be alert to the reality of spiritual warfare, and fight it in the biblical (and only effective) way. I need to be protected myself and to be able to help others understand how they can be protected.

On the other hand, a spiritual-warfare–model counselor gave impressive statistics from his own experience of people who have been dramatically helped almost overnight from conditions that typical counseling takes months and years to help, and sometimes cannot help at all.

As a pastor, I have no vested interest in either approach for its own sake. I am interested in a functional scriptural approach. I think both may be useful, depending on the individual needing help. As a result, I think it is possible to integrate the two models to a much greater degree than is usually done. I prefer an integrated approach, combining the strengths of both schools of thought.

First, it is necessary to eliminate as much as possible the likelihood that physical problems are the source of the emotional or mental problems. Low blood sugar, chemical imbalance in the blood, vitamin and/or mineral deficiencies, thyroid malfunction, poor circulation, and a host of other physical problems can cause depression, anxiety, emotional instability, and/or mental agitation. Perhaps the first and most important step is to try to eliminate any physical origin for the mental or emotional problems.

Medications are closely related to this principle. Something as simple and seemingly harmless as antihistamines and decongestants can cause a person to be angry, irritable, anxious, or depressed, and to cry easily or lose sleep. Other stronger medications can have the same or worse reactions. It is very frustrating and self-defeating for people to be probing your soul for spiritual or emotional problems when the cause is a physical problem or medication.

It is helpful to find a doctor who is alert to this principle. Physicians sometimes do not spot subtle physical problems, particularly those that are related to the meteoric rise in allergy and environmental illnesses that many physicians are unaware of or dismiss altogether. It can be very difficult to eliminate physical problems if your symptoms are troublesome, but be sure to give sufficient attention to the physical side of things.

Second, I believe it is important to be sure the person needing help is a Christian. If he isn't, that doesn't mean you can't help him. Many people are won to Christ in a counselor's office. But it does mean that your ability to help him in spiritual warfare is limited until he does become a Christian.

Third, when he does become a Christian, he must understand who he has become in Christ. Unless a person has an accurate understanding of his new birth, his new identity, his new being, his new inner power, he is not likely to benefit fully from counseling.

Fourth, a person must understand the necessity of holiness in everyday living. Holiness does not mean you never sin. If that were what it meant, no one except Jesus would be holy. Rather, the secret to holiness is ready repentance of sin when the Holy Spirit convicts you of it. No one will ever stop sinning altogether. But if a person will repent of the sin when he sees what he has done or not done, and will allow the Lord to restore him to fellowship, he can live a holy life. Holiness is not for just a select few; all Christians are called to holiness.

Fifth, since a counselor cannot take another person beyond the counselor's own level of spiritual maturity, the number one characteristic of the counselor must be Christlikeness, not merely a degree on a wall or some special technique.

Sixth, the counselor must understand the centrality of a cleansed conscience to the process. Until a person is willing to make a complete commitment to cleansing his conscience, counseling can have only a limited impact.

Seventh, a support group or discipleship arrangement needs to be created to help the counselees sustain their commitments. Counseling must get the counselee involved in other persons' lives sooner or later, or else life change will rarely be sustained. God never intended for us to be able to make it alone. Counseling without eventually requiring local church involvement misses an essential ingredient of wholeness.

All this can be done by lay counselors and disciplers. If, after going through this process, a person still needs professional counseling, it should be from someone who understands and embraces the above process. If, by the time a person got to a professional counselor he had reached an understanding of who he is in Christ and of what holiness is and had cleansed his conscience and was involved in some kind of a small group or discipleship relationship, he would be well on his way to benefiting from all the additional help the professional biblical counselor could give.

There might be reasons why this exact procedure would not be followed with some people. However, if this were a general approach used with discernment and discretion, I believe the greatest number of people would be helped by the most efficient use of resources within the church.

It has been my observation that unless a person understands the truth of who he is in Christ and is obedient to it by cleansing his conscience and committing to a life of righteousness, he will not be set free from emotional bondage. Even if a person understands truth and is willing to obey it, he may need to be nurtured through a process of assimilating truth and intensifying obedience.

> **The unrepentant person will not be healed.**

However, it has been my observation that much of the psychological-model counseling tries to go right to the problem and fix it without laying a proper foundation for improvement. Much of this kind of counseling does not take into account the potential presence of demons, the need to cleanse the conscience, or the need for personal involvement in worship services and small-group or discipleship relationships, along with the spiritual disciplines of prayer, fellowship, Bible reading and study, and so forth. I have witnessed too many people who have gone through psychological counseling and were never expected or held accountable to do the things that encourage emotional and spiritual health. Too much emphasis is placed on psychological therapies not integrated with spiritual therapy.

In addition, I have seen people go through months and even years of counseling with little result. I think, in too many cases, that repentance was not sufficiently emphasized. A person who will not repent will not be healed. I also think, in some cases, that counselors who are not spiritually mature try to help by using only a counseling model learned in a secular classroom. In such cases, well-meaning counselors are trying to impart something (a truly spiritual therapy) they themselves have not experienced. It doesn't work.

On the other hand, I have seen spiritual-warfare counselors try to cast demons out of people when the problems seemed transparently not to be demonic in origin.

Too many spiritual-warfare counselors have only one bullet in their gun: get rid of the demons. If that doesn't work, some have little to offer.

I believe the body of Christ would be significantly helped by the two disciplines complementing each other and adopting a model that uses both approaches in enlightened cooperation with one another.

CONCLUSION

As I said earlier, the goal of Satan and his demons is to deceive us in order to destroy us. In years past, overt demon activity was comparatively rare in the United States because the societal mind-set was more overtly Christian and very much against demonic things. In such times, Satan's strategy was to come to us as an angel of light (2 Corinthians 11:14). He came to us, I believe, in the guise of intellectual sophistication. The result has been the acceptance of the theory of evolution, the repudiation of the truth of Scripture followed by the rejection of the deity of Christ and the Holy Spirit and the denial of the sinfulness of humanity and its need for personal salvation. Removing God as much as possible from all public forums followed and science was elevated to the level of generally accepted truth. Whatever a minister said was suspect. Whatever a scientist said was true. Satan used these subtle, "angel of light" tactics early in our history as a nation up into the twentieth century.

> **As light in the culture dims, darkness advances.**

These "harmless" decisions, however, began to bear their fruit. Removing God as the authority over our society left every person free to do what was right in his own eyes. The result has been an unprecedented collapse of moral values, profound disruption in the integrity of our educational, judicial, and governmental systems, a tidal wave of crime, and a disintegration of the cultural standards that welded us together as a nation. The angel of light began to dim.

These sudden and profound changes have now spawned a subculture of people who readily accept the devil as an angel of darkness, which is his true identity. Musical groups with names like Slayer and Carcass sing songs such as "Under the Rotted Flesh," "Covered with Sores," and "Raining Blood." An album came out entitled *Butchered at Birth*, with graphic pictures of mutilated babies. This kind of music is called death metal, and albums are selling by the hundreds of thousands. Glorifying blood, violence, and satanism lets you peek inside the door of hell. If you want to look at what hell is like, these things give you a glimpse.

People who listen to this kind of music also do other unspeakable things. Chuck Colson reported that when a television talk show recently ran a program about children who had committed murder, everyone said they listened to death metal music (*A Dangerous Grace*, 252).

As light dims, darkness advances. Spiritually in America, the light is dimming and darkness is advancing. Things we once regarded as unthinkable are now commonplace. And this has happened in my adult lifetime, a stunningly brief period of time.

We must now fight the spiritual warfare on many fronts. We must fight the "angel of light" kind of tactics, in which Satan uses science, education, political correctness, and so forth to bring about an agenda that is touted as good. Some of it may be. That's part of the deception. But also we must fight overt Satan worship in all its hideousness—and we must fight everything in between.

Learning the biblical basics of spiritual warfare is just the beginning. The battle will only spread and intensify. We have the resources, the truth, and the power for personal victory. We must shield ourselves and our loved ones by following God's strategy. And we must try to take back ground lost in our society by manifesting the character of Christ and proclaiming His name.

Onward Christian soldiers!

SPEED BUMP!

Slow down to be sure you have gotten the main points of this chapter.

Q1. Can Christians be influenced by demons?

A1. Christians can be influenced by demons, so we must always be *on guard* spiritually.

Q2. How can we be protected from the forces of darkness?

A2. We can be protected from the forces of darkness by a life of *obedience* to the Scripture and of trusting God to protect us.

Q3. Should Christians cast demons out of others?

A3. Believers are not all agreed on whether or not exorcisms are valid, but they do agree that lasting liberty for demonized persons depends on their *cooperation.*

Q4. How can we help others in the spiritual war?

A4. We can help others in the spiritual war by taking them through a process of cleansing their conscience and using prayer and Scripture to *resist* demonic influence.

FILL IN THE BLANK

Q1. Can Christians be influenced by demons?

A1. Christians can be influenced by demons, so we must always be _____ spiritually.

Q2. How can we be protected from the forces of darkness?

A2. We can be protected from the forces of darkness by a life of _____ to the Scripture and of trusting God to protect us.

Q3. Should Christians cast demons out of others?

A3. Believers are not all agreed on whether or not exorcisms are valid, but they do agree that lasting liberty for demonized persons depends on their _____.

Q4. How can we help others in the spiritual war?

A4. We can help others in the spiritual war by taking them through a process of cleansing their conscience and using prayer and Scripture to _____ demonic influence.

FOR FURTHER THOUGHT AND DISCUSSION

1. Are you confident that you have done everything you need to do to be secure from demonic influence? If not, what do you think you should do?

2. Do you know anyone whom you think might be struggling with demonization? What do you think you could do to help that person?

3. Do you think any activities you are involved in are making you susceptible to demonic influence? Think through your music, television, movies, reading, friends, interests, hobbies. Is there anything you think you need to eliminate from your life?

WHAT IF I DON'T BELIEVE?

1. If I don't believe, I may do things that may encourage demonic activity in my life.

2. I may think that I am able to take care of myself and, in doing so, be deceived by demons.

3. I may not follow a dependable route to help if I am struggling with demonic activity in my life.

4. I may not take seriously enough the alarming escalation in things today that encourage demonic activity.

5. If I am a parent, I may not give my child(ren) the guidance necessary to protect them from demonic activity in their lives.

FOR FURTHER STUDY

1. Scripture

Several Scripture passages speak of the need to stand firm in spiritual warfare:

- 1 Corinthians 6:9
- 1 Corinthians 5:1–5
- 2 Corinthians 5:17
- 1 John 1:7
- 1 John 4:4

2. Books

Several other books are very helpful in studying this subject further. They are listed below according to the view they support. They are the same books recommended after chapter 1:

1. Spiritual Resistance View:
   How to Meet the Enemy, John MacArthur
   Spiritual Warfare, Ray Stedman

2. Truth Encounter View
   The Bondage Breaker, Neil Anderson
   Victory over the Darkness, Neil Anderson

3. Power Encounter View
   The Adversary, Mark Bubeck
   The Handbook for Spiritual Warfare, Ed Murphy

BIBLIOGRAPHY

Anderson, Neil. *Released from Bondage.* Nashville: Thomas Nelson, 1991.

Colson, Chuck. *A Dangerous Grace.* Dallas: Word, 1994.

Graham, Billy. *Angels: God's Secret Agents.* Dallas: Word, 1986.

McClelland, S. E. "Demon, Demon Possession." *Evangelical Dictionary of Theology.* Walter Elwell, ed. Grand Rapids: Baker, 1984.

Poole, Rebecca. "Uganda's Wild Child," *Sierra*, January/February 1987.

"Ready for Something Tremendous!" *Christianity Today*, December 14, 1992:11.

Richmond, Gary. *A View from the Zoo.* Dallas: Word, 1986.

Spurgeon, Charles Haddon. *Morning and Evening.* Roy Clarke, ed. Nashville: Thomas Nelson, 1994.

Tada, Joni Eareckson. *A Step Further.* Grand Rapids: Zondervan, 1998.

White, John. *The Fight.* Downer's Grove, IL: InterVarsity, 1976.

MASTER REVIEW

Chapter 1

Q1. What are the three battlefronts in spiritual warfare?

A1. The three battlefronts in our spiritual warfare are the world, the flesh, and the *devil*.

Q2. What is the source of our strength?

A2. The source of our strength in the spiritual war is *God* alone.

Q3. What are the weapons of war?

A3. Our weapons of war are the pieces of spiritual *armor* described in Scripture.

Q4. What are Satan's methods of deception?

A4. Satan employs two particularly effective means of deceiving us: first he gets us to sin; then, once we have sinned, he keeps us mired in *guilt*.

Q5. How can we get the power to overcome?

A5. We are able to overcome Satan by realizing that his only power over us is that of deception and fear, and by *resisting* him God's way.

Q6. What are three primary perspectives on spiritual warfare?

A6. The three primary perspectives on spiritual warfare are the Spiritual *Resistance* View, the *Truth* Encounter View, and the *Power* Encounter View.

Chapter 2

Q1. What are good angels?

A1. Angels are *spirits* who live mostly in an unseen realm and do the will of God.

Q2. Who is Satan?

A2. Satan, probably the highest good angel before he rebelled against God, is now the *enemy* who opposes the will of God.

Q3. What are demons?

A3. Demons are probably the angels who *sinned* by following Satan in his rebellion against God. They now oppose the will of God and do the will of Satan.

Chapter 3

Q1. What does the belt of truth picture?

A1. The belt of truth pictures a *commitment* to the truth of the Word of God.

Q2. What must our level of commitment to truth be?

A2. Our commitment to truth must be *total* and unending.

Q3. Why must a Christian tell the truth in word and in deed?

A3. The Christian must tell the truth in word and deed, or else his character, the *credibility* of the gospel, and the reputation of God, Himself, are compromised.

Q4. Is truth absolute or relative?

A4. God's truth is *absolute*, eternal, and unchanging.

Chapter 4

Q1. What does the breastplate of righteousness picture?

A1. The breastplate of righteousness pictures a *lifestyle* of trusting obedience to God.

Q2. What are the two dimensions of righteousness?

A2. Righteousness is both *imputed* and *imparted*.

Q3. How do we put on the breastplate of daily righteous living?

A3. We don the breastplate of daily righteous living by being faithfully *obedient* to all we understand Christ is asking of us.

Q4. How does sin hurt us?

A4. Sin hurts us by inflicting predictably painful *consequences*.

Chapter 5

Q1. What do the shoes of the gospel of peace picture?

A1. The shoes of the gospel of peace picture a trusting confidence in the *promises* of God, and the sense of peace that such trust brings.

Q2. How do God's promises give us peace?

A2. God's promises give us peace by answering our greatest *fears*.

Q3. How do God's promises lighten our load?

A3. God's promises lighten our load by helping us lay down *burdens* that God never intended us to carry.

Chapter 6

Q1. What does the shield of faith picture?

A1. The shield of faith pictures a life of protection based on our *faith* in God's character, word, and deeds.

Q2. What is faith?

A2. Faith is *believing* what God has said and *committing* ourselves to His Word.

Q3. What are the flaming arrows?

A3. The Bible does not tell us specifically what Satan's flaming arrows are, though they can be anything that causes us to *doubt* or disobey the truth.

Q4. How do we use the shield of faith?

A4. We use the shield of faith when we *commit* ourselves to live according to the truth of God's Word instead of Satan's lies.

Chapter 7

Q1. What does the helmet of salvation picture?

A1. The helmet of salvation pictures a lifestyle of *hope* that comes from focusing on our ultimate salvation.

Q2. How do we cultivate an eternal perspective?

A2. We cultivate an eternal perspective by viewing all temporal things in light of *eternity.*

Q3. How do I transfer my hope from this world to the next?

A3. I transfer my hope from this world to the next by using the disappointments of this world as a catalyst to consciously *embrace* God's answer to those disappointments.

Chapter 8

Q1. What does the sword of the Spirit picture?

A1. The sword of the Spirit pictures an offensive and defensive use of the *Bible* in spiritual warfare.

Q2. How is the sword used for defense?

A2. The sword is used *defensively* by applying Scripture to every doubt, temptation, and discouragement hurled at us by Satan.

Q3. How is the sword used for offense?

A3. The sword is used *offensively* to cause change, encouraging spiritual growth through evangelism, teaching, preaching, and counseling.

Chapter 9

Q1. How do we make contact with our Commander?

A1. In the spiritual war, we make contact with our Commander through *prayer.*

Q2. How do we get a response from our Commander?

A2. We get a response from our Commander by praying according to the *guidelines* given us in Scripture.

Q3. Why do we foster a relationship with our Commander?

A3. We foster a relationship with our Commander because our *relationship* with God is even more important than a specific answer to a given prayer.

Chapter 10

Q1. How does God see us?

A1. God sees us *in Christ*, having been born again in righteousness and true holiness in spirit, awaiting our complete adoption, the redemption of our bodies.

Q2. What should our response be to our new identity in Christ?

A2. Our response should be *gratitude* and obedience.

Chapter 11

Q1. What is a clear conscience?

A1. A clear conscience is one free of guilt, not because we've never sinned, but because we've responded *biblically* to our sin.

Q2. How can we gain a clear conscience?

A2. We can gain a clear conscience by *repenting* of known sin, forgiving those who've wronged us, and seeking forgiveness from those we have wronged.

Q3. How can we protect our conscience from evil influences and pull down spiritual strongholds?

A3. We can protect our conscience from evil influences by repenting from and *renouncing* anything we may be doing or may have done in the past that has made us vulnerable to demonic influence.

Chapter 12

Q1. Can Christians be influenced by demons?

A1. Christians can be influenced by demons, so we must always be *on guard* spiritually.

Q2. How can we be protected from the forces of darkness?

A2. We can be protected from the forces of darkness by a life of *obedience* to the Scripture and of trusting God to protect us.

Q3. Should Christians cast demons out of others?

A3. Believers are not all agreed on whether or not exorcisms are valid, but they do agree that lasting liberty for demonized persons depends on their *cooperation*.

Q4. How can we help others in the spiritual war?

A4. We can help others in the spiritual war by taking them through a process of cleansing their conscience and using prayer and Scripture to *resist* demonic influence.

ABOUT THE AUTHOR

Max Anders (Th.M. Dallas Theological Seminary, D. Min Western Seminary) is the author of over twenty books and the creator and general editor of the thirty-two-volume Holman Bible Commentary. Dr. Anders has taught on the college and seminary level, was one of the original team members with Walk Thru the Bible Ministries, and has pastored for over twenty years. He is the founder and president of 7 Marks, Inc., a ministry specializing in discipleship strategies and materials for local churches (www.7marks.org). His book *30 Days to Understanding the Bible* has reached more than 300,000 readers with a passion for learning God's Word.